MEDITERRANEAN DIET COOKBOOK FOR BEGINNERS

Expert Tips for a Vibrant Lifestyle, 150 Simple Recipes, Nutritional Information for Health and Wellness, 30 Day Meal Plans

WINONA OLSON

Disclaimer

This cookbook is intended for informational and educational purposes only. The recipes and dietary suggestions provided are based on the author's personal experiences and research. While every effort has been made to ensure the accuracy of the information, the author makes no guarantees regarding its applicability to individual circumstances.

Consult a healthcare professional or a registered dietitian before making significant changes to your diet, especially if you have any pre-existing health conditions or dietary restrictions. The author shall not be held liable for any adverse effects or consequences resulting from the use or application of the information and recipes contained in this book.

By using this cookbook, you acknowledge and accept that you are responsible for your dietary choices and health decisions.

Table of contents

CHAPTER 5: GRAINS, PASTA, AND RICE RECIPES   38

CHAPTER 6: FISH AND SEAFOOD   47

CHAPTER 7: POULTY RECIPES   56

CHAPTER 8: MEAT RECIPES   67

CHAPTER 9: VEGETABLE RECIPES   79

CHAPTER 10: DESSERTS   87

CHAPTER 1

EMBRACING THE MEDITERRANEAN DIET: A GATEWAY TO HEALTH AND VITALITY

The Mediterranean Diet is a celebrated way of eating that originates from the culinary traditions of countries bordering the Mediterranean Sea, such as Greece, Italy, and Spain. Recognized for its flavorful dishes and nutritional benefits, this diet emphasizes whole foods, healthy fats, and a lifestyle that values community and activity. By understanding its foundational principles and health benefits, individuals can find motivation to embrace this sustainable way of eating, leading to improved health and well-being.

Foundational Principles and Key Food Groups

At the core of the Mediterranean Diet are foundational principles that focus on balance, variety, and moderation. The diet primarily includes:

- **Fruits and Vegetables** - a cornerstone of the Mediterranean diet, these should make up a significant portion of daily meals. They provide essential vitamins, minerals, fiber, and antioxidants, contributing to overall health.
- **Whole Grains** - foods such as whole grain bread, brown rice, quinoa, and oats are preferred over refined grains. Whole grains are high in fiber, aiding digestion and providing long-lasting energy.
- **Healthy Fats** - the primary source of fat is olive oil, known for its heart-healthy monounsaturated fats. Other sources include nuts, seeds, and avocados, which contribute to heart health and satiety.
- **Lean Proteins** - fish and seafood are eaten regularly, providing omega-3 fatty acids, while poultry and eggs are consumed in moderation. Red meat is limited, allowing for a focus on plant-based proteins like legumes and beans.
- **Dairy** - moderate consumption of dairy, particularly yogurt and cheese, adds beneficial probiotics and calcium to the diet.
- **Herbs and Spices** -these are used generously to enhance flavor, reducing the need for salt and adding health benefits through their antioxidant properties.
- **Social and Physical Activity** - the Mediterranean lifestyle encourages regular physical activity and enjoying meals with family and friends, both of which contribute to overall well-being.

These principles not only promote a nutrient-rich diet but also foster healthy habits that can lead to improved energy levels and disease prevention.

Health Benefits of the Mediterranean Diet

Research consistently supports the health benefits associated with the Mediterranean Diet, making it a credible choice for those seeking a healthier lifestyle.

1. **Heart Health**: numerous studies have shown that the Mediterranean Diet can reduce the risk of cardiovascular diseases. For instance, a landmark study published in *The New England Journal of Medicine* demonstrated that participants adhering to this diet had a lower incidence of heart attacks and strokes compared to those following a low-fat diet.

2. **Weight Management**: the Mediterranean Diet is linked to effective weight management. By emphasizing whole foods and fiber-rich options, it helps individuals feel fuller for longer. Research published in *Obesity* indicates that this diet can be more effective than low-fat diets for weight loss and maintenance.
3. **Diabetes Prevention and Management**: the diet's focus on low glycemic index foods helps regulate blood sugar levels, making it beneficial for individuals with type 2 diabetes or those at risk. A study in *Diabetes Care* found that individuals following the Mediterranean Diet had better glycemic control and improved insulin sensitivity.
4. **Cognitive Benefits**: the Mediterranean Diet has been associated with a reduced risk of cognitive decline and Alzheimer's disease. The presence of antioxidants in fruits, vegetables, and healthy fats supports brain health. A study in *Frontiers in Nutrition* concluded that adherence to this diet was linked to improved cognitive function in older adults.
5. **Longevity**: research published in *BMJ* highlights that following the Mediterranean Diet is associated with increased life expectancy. The diet's anti-inflammatory properties contribute to reducing chronic disease risk, leading to a longer, healthier life.

Mental and Emotional Benefits

Beyond its physical health advantages, the Mediterranean Diet offers significant mental and emotional benefits. The balanced nutrition can lead to improved mood and emotional well-being. Foods rich in omega-3 fatty acids and antioxidants support brain health, potentially reducing symptoms of depression and anxiety.

Additionally, the communal aspect of dining, common in Mediterranean cultures, fosters social connections. Sharing meals with loved ones enhances emotional bonds and reduces feelings of isolation, which can positively impact mental health. Many individuals report experiencing better sleep patterns and increased energy levels after adopting this way of eating, contributing to an overall sense of well-being.

Real-Life Transformations

Many individuals have successfully transitioned to the Mediterranean Diet and witnessed significant improvements in their health and quality of life. For example, Sarah, a 52-year-old teacher, struggled with weight management and fatigue. After adopting the Mediterranean Diet, she lost 15 pounds, experienced increased energy, and reported a notable improvement in her mood. The emphasis on fresh foods and cooking at home reignited her passion for cooking and eating, making her meals more enjoyable.

Similarly, David, a 60-year-old retiree, was diagnosed with high cholesterol. After shifting to the Mediterranean Diet, he saw his cholesterol levels drop significantly within three months. He embraced the lifestyle changes not just for his health but also for the joy of preparing meals using vibrant ingredients and sharing them with family.

Practical Tips for Incorporation

Integrating the Mediterranean Diet into daily life can be simple and enjoyable. Here are some practical tips:

1. Start by planning meals for the week that incorporate a variety of fruits, vegetables, whole grains, and lean proteins. Focus on preparing one or two vegetarian meals each week.

2. Create a shopping list emphasizing fresh, seasonal produce, whole grains, and healthy fats. Explore local farmers' markets for fresher ingredients.
3. Opt for cooking methods such as grilling, baking, steaming, or sautéing with olive oil instead of frying. Experiment with herbs and spices to add flavor without excess salt.
4. When eating out, choose restaurants that offer Mediterranean-inspired dishes. Look for options like grilled fish, fresh salads, and whole grain sides. Don't hesitate to request modifications to suit your dietary preferences.

Adopting the Mediterranean Diet is more than a dietary change; it is a sustainable lifestyle choice that fosters long-term health benefits. By focusing on whole foods, engaging in social dining experiences, and prioritizing physical activity, individuals can enhance their quality of life and well-being.

Embrace the Mediterranean way of eating not just for its health benefits but for the joy of flavorful meals shared with loved ones. This diet invites you to savor each bite, explore new recipes, and cultivate a vibrant, healthy lifestyle. Let the Mediterranean Diet be your pathway to a healthier, more fulfilling life, where every meal is an opportunity for joy and connection.

CHAPTER 2: BREAKFAST

Mediterranean Spinach and Feta Omelette

Yield: 2 servings
Preparation Time: 5 minutes
Cooking Time: 10 minutes

Ingredients:

- 4 large eggs
- 1 cup fresh spinach, chopped
- 1/2 cup feta cheese, crumbled
- 1 tablespoon olive oil
- 1/4 cup red onion, finely chopped
- Salt and pepper to taste
- Optional: 1 tablespoon fresh dill or parsley, chopped

Instructions:

1. In a bowl, whisk together the eggs, salt, and pepper, and set aside.
2. Heat olive oil in a non-stick skillet over medium heat, then add the red onion and sauté for 2-3 minutes until softened.
3. Add the chopped spinach and cook until wilted, about 1-2 minutes, then pour in the whisked eggs, swirling the skillet to ensure even coverage.
4. Sprinkle the crumbled feta cheese on top and cook for about 3-4 minutes until the edges are set, then fold the omelette in half and cook for another minute.
5. Serve immediately, garnished with fresh herbs if desired.

Nutritional Information (per serving):
- **Calories:** *250*
- **Protein:** *18g*
- **Carbohydrates:** *4g*
- **Fats:** *18g*
- **Fiber:** *1g*
- **Cholesterol:** *400mg*
- **Sodium:** *550mg*
- **Potassium:** *400mg*

Greek Yogurt and Honey Parfait

Yield: 2 servings
Preparation Time: 10 minutes
Cooking Time: 0 minutes

Ingredients:
- 2 cups Greek yogurt (plain, unsweetened)
- 4 tablespoons honey
- 1 cup mixed berries (strawberries, blueberries, raspberries)
- 1/2 cup granola (preferably whole grain)
- Optional: 1 tablespoon chopped nuts (almonds or walnuts)

Instructions:
1. In a bowl, layer half of the Greek yogurt at the bottom of two glasses or bowls.
2. Drizzle 2 tablespoons of honey over the yogurt, then add half of the mixed berries on top.
3. Sprinkle 1/4 cup of granola over the berries, then repeat the layers with the remaining yogurt, honey, and berries.
4. Top each parfait with the remaining granola and optional chopped nuts, and garnish with fresh mint leaves if desired.
5. Serve immediately for a refreshing and nutritious breakfast or snack.

Nutritional Information (per serving):
- **Calories:** *280*
- **Protein:** *18g*
- **Carbohydrates:** *40g*
- **Fats:** *6g*
- **Fiber:** *4g*
- **Cholesterol:** *10mg*
- **Sodium:** *75mg*
- **Potassium:** *400mg*

Za'atar-Spiced Breakfast Pita

Yield: 2 servings
Preparation Time: 10 minutes
Cooking Time: 5 minutes

Ingredients:

- 2 whole wheat pitas
- 1 cup eggs (about 2 large eggs)
- 1 tablespoon za'atar spice blend
- 1/2 cup cherry tomatoes, halved
- 1/4 cup feta cheese, crumbled
- 2 tablespoons olive oil
- Salt and pepper, to taste
- Optional: Fresh parsley or mint for garnish

Instructions:

1. In a small bowl, whisk together the eggs, za'atar spice, salt, and pepper until well combined.
2. Heat 1 tablespoon of olive oil in a skillet over medium heat, then pour in the egg mixture, stirring gently until the eggs are just set.
3. Meanwhile, warm the pitas in another skillet or directly over an open flame for about 1 minute until soft and pliable.
4. Once the eggs are cooked, divide them between the warmed pitas and top with cherry tomatoes and crumbled feta cheese.
5. Drizzle the remaining olive oil over the top, garnish with fresh herbs if using, and serve immediately.

Nutritional Information (per serving):

- *Calories:* 290
- *Protein:* 14g
- *Carbohydrates:* 28g
- *Fats:* 15g
- *Fiber:* 5g
- *Cholesterol:* 250mg
- *Sodium:* 500mg
- *Potassium:* 400mg

Shakshuka with Fresh Herbs

Yield: 4 servings
Preparation Time: 10 minutes
Cooking Time: 20 minutes

Ingredients:

- 2 tablespoons olive oil
- 1 onion, finely chopped
- 2 garlic cloves, minced
- 1 red bell pepper, chopped
- 1 can (14 oz) diced tomatoes (or 4 fresh tomatoes, chopped)
- 1 teaspoon ground cumin
- 1 teaspoon smoked paprika
- Salt and pepper, to taste
- 4 large eggs
- 1/4 cup fresh parsley, chopped (or cilantro)
- 1/4 cup fresh basil, chopped (optional)

Instructions:

1. Heat the olive oil in a large skillet over medium heat; add the onion and red bell pepper, sautéing until softened, about 5 minutes.
2. Stir in the garlic, cumin, smoked paprika, salt, and pepper, cooking for an additional minute until fragrant.
3. Add the diced tomatoes, reduce the heat, and simmer for 10 minutes until the sauce thickens slightly.
4. Create small wells in the sauce and crack an egg into each well; cover and cook until the eggs are set to your liking, about 5–7 minutes.
5. Remove from heat, sprinkle with fresh herbs and feta if desired, and serve hot with crusty bread or pita.

Nutritional Information (per serving):

- *Calories:* 220
- *Protein:* 11g
- *Carbohydrates:* 10g
- *Fats:* 16g
- *Fiber:* 3g
- *Cholesterol:* 215mg
- *Sodium:* 350mg
- *Potassium:* 400mg

Lemon Ricotta Pancakes with Berries

Yield: 4 servings (about 8 pancakes)
Preparation Time: 10 minutes
Cooking Time: 15 minutes

Ingredients:

- **For the Pancakes:**
    - 1 cup ricotta cheese
    - 2 large eggs
    - 1/2 cup all-purpose flour (or whole wheat flour)
    - 1 tablespoon baking powder
    - Zest of 1 lemon
    - 2 tablespoons lemon juice
    - 1 tablespoon honey or maple syrup (optional)
    - Pinch of salt
- **For the Topping:**
    - 1 cup mixed berries (strawberries, blueberries, raspberries)
    - 1 tablespoon honey (optional)
    - Fresh mint leaves (for garnish, optional)

Instructions:

1. In a large bowl, whisk together the ricotta, eggs, lemon zest, lemon juice, and honey (if using) until smooth.
2. In a separate bowl, combine the flour, baking powder, and salt; then fold the dry ingredients into the ricotta mixture until just combined.
3. Heat a non-stick skillet or griddle over medium heat and lightly grease it; pour 1/4 cup of batter for each pancake, cooking until bubbles form on the surface, about 2-3 minutes, then flip and cook for an additional 2 minutes until golden.
4. Meanwhile, toss the mixed berries with honey if desired to enhance their sweetness.
5. Serve the pancakes warm, topped with the berry mixture and fresh mint leaves, if using.

Nutritional Information (per serving):

- *Calories:* 220
- *Protein:* 9g
- *Carbohydrates:* 25g
- *Fats:* 9g
- *Fiber:* 3g
- *Cholesterol:* 70mg
- *Sodium:* 170mg
- *Potassium:* 250mg

Avocado and Hummus Toast

Yield: 2 servings
Preparation Time: 10 minutes
Cooking Time: 0 minutes

Ingredients:

- 2 slices whole-grain or sourdough bread
- 1 ripe avocado
- 1/2 cup hummus (store-bought or homemade)
- 1 tablespoon olive oil
- Juice of 1/2 lemon
- Salt and pepper, to taste
- Optional toppings: cherry tomatoes, radishes, cucumber slices, red pepper flakes, fresh herbs (e.g., parsley, cilantro)

Instructions:

1. Toast the whole-grain or sourdough bread slices until golden brown.
2. In a bowl, mash the avocado with olive oil, lemon juice, salt, and pepper until smooth but still chunky.
3. Spread a generous layer of hummus on each slice of toasted bread.
4. Top each toast with the mashed avocado mixture and any additional toppings you like (e.g., sliced cherry tomatoes, cucumber, or radishes).
5. Drizzle with extra olive oil and sprinkle with red pepper flakes or fresh herbs if desired.

Nutritional Information (per serving):

- *Calories: 310*
- *Protein: 10g*
- *Carbohydrates: 32g*
- *Fats: 17g*
- *Fiber: 10g*
- *Cholesterol: 0mg*
- *Sodium: 240mg*
- *Potassium: 600mg*

Olive Oil Fried Eggs with Spinach and Tomatoes

Yield: 2 servings
Preparation Time: 5 minutes
Cooking Time: 10 minutes

Ingredients:

- 4 large eggs
- 2 tablespoons extra-virgin olive oil
- 2 cups fresh spinach, washed and dried
- 1 cup cherry tomatoes, halved
- 1 clove garlic, minced
- Salt and pepper, to taste
- Optional: Feta cheese, fresh herbs (e.g., basil or parsley) for garnish

Instructions:

1. Heat the olive oil in a large skillet over medium heat; add the minced garlic and sauté until fragrant, about 1 minute.
2. Add the cherry tomatoes and cook for 2-3 minutes until they begin to soften, then add the spinach and cook until wilted, about 1-2 minutes.
3. Push the vegetables to the side of the skillet and crack the eggs into the pan, seasoning with salt and pepper.
4. Cook the eggs to your desired doneness (sunny-side up or over-easy), about 3-5 minutes.
5. Serve the eggs over the sautéed spinach and tomatoes, garnished with feta cheese and fresh herbs if desired.

Nutritional Information (per serving):

- *Calories: 300*
- *Protein: 15g*
- *Carbohydrates: 6g*
- *Fats: 24g*
- *Fiber: 2g*
- *Cholesterol: 370mg*
- *Sodium: 300mg*
- *Potassium: 550mg*

Labneh with Pistachios and Pomegranate

Yield: *4 servings*
Preparation Time: *10 minutes*
Cooking Time: *0 minutes (chilling time not included)*

Ingredients:

- 2 cups plain yogurt (preferably Greek or strained)
- 1/4 teaspoon salt
- 1/4 cup unsalted pistachios, roughly chopped
- 1/2 cup pomegranate seeds
- 1 tablespoon extra-virgin olive oil
- Optional: fresh mint leaves for garnish

Instructions:

1. In a bowl, mix the yogurt and salt, then strain it through a cheesecloth or fine mesh sieve for 2-3 hours to thicken.
2. Transfer the strained yogurt (labneh) to a serving dish, creating a shallow well in the center.
3. Drizzle the olive oil into the well and sprinkle the chopped pistachios and pomegranate seeds evenly on top.
4. Garnish with fresh mint leaves if desired and additional salt to taste.
5. Serve with pita bread or fresh vegetables for dipping.

Nutritional Information (per serving):

- *Calories: 150*
- *Protein: 6g*
- *Carbohydrates: 12g*
- *Fats: 10g*
- *Fiber: 2g*
- *Cholesterol: 5mg*
- *Sodium: 110mg*
- *Potassium: 210mg*

Smoked Salmon Breakfast Bagel

Yield: *2 servings*
Preparation Time: *10 minutes*
Cooking Time: *0 minutes*

Ingredients:

- 2 whole grain bagels, halved
- 1/2 cup cream cheese (or Greek yogurt for a lighter option)
- 4 ounces smoked salmon
- 1/2 small red onion, thinly sliced
- 1/2 cup cucumber, thinly sliced
- 1 tablespoon capers (optional)
- Fresh dill or chives for garnish
- Optional: lemon wedges for serving

Instructions:

1. Toast the bagel halves until golden brown.
2. Spread cream cheese or Greek yogurt evenly on each bagel half.
3. Layer the smoked salmon on top, followed by red onion slices, cucumber, and capers if using.
4. Garnish with fresh dill or chives, and a squeeze of lemon juice if desired.
5. Serve immediately and enjoy as a nutritious breakfast or brunch option.

Nutritional Information (per serving):

- *Calories: 350*
- *Protein: 20g*
- *Carbohydrates: 40g*
- *Fats: 14g*
- *Fiber: 5g*
- *Cholesterol: 50mg*
- *Sodium: 750mg*
- *Potassium: 600mg*

Mediterranean Breakfast Burrito

Yield: 2 servings
Preparation Time: 10 minutes
Cooking Time: 10 minutes

Ingredients:

- 4 large eggs
- 1/4 cup milk (or almond milk)
- 1/2 cup cooked spinach, chopped
- 1/4 cup cherry tomatoes, halved
- 1/4 cup feta cheese, crumbled
- 1/4 cup olives, sliced (black or green)
- 2 whole wheat tortillas
- 1 tablespoon olive oil
- Salt and pepper to taste
- Fresh parsley or basil for garnish

Instructions:

1. In a bowl, whisk together the eggs, milk, salt, and pepper.
2. Heat olive oil in a skillet over medium heat, add the egg mixture, and scramble until just set, then add spinach, tomatoes, feta, and olives.
3. Warm the tortillas in a separate skillet for about 30 seconds on each side.
4. Divide the egg mixture evenly between the tortillas, roll them up tightly, and slice in half.
5. Garnish with fresh parsley or basil and serve immediately.

Nutritional Information (per serving):

- *Calories: 350*
- *Protein: 18g*
- *Carbohydrates: 35g*
- *Fats: 15g*
- *Fiber: 4g*
- *Cholesterol: 200mg*
- *Sodium: 650mg*
- *Potassium: 600mg*

Roasted Red Pepper and Goat Cheese Frittata

Yield: 4 servings
Preparation Time: 10 minutes
Cooking Time: 25 minutes

Ingredients:

- 6 large eggs
- 1/4 cup milk (or almond milk)
- 1 cup roasted red peppers, chopped
- 1/2 cup goat cheese, crumbled
- 1/4 cup onion, finely chopped
- 1 tablespoon olive oil
- Salt and pepper to taste
- Fresh basil or parsley for garnish

Instructions:

1. Preheat the oven to 375°F (190°C) and heat olive oil in an oven-safe skillet over medium heat; sauté the onion until softened, about 3 minutes.
2. In a bowl, whisk together the eggs, milk, salt, and pepper, then fold in the roasted red peppers and goat cheese.
3. Pour the egg mixture into the skillet and cook for 5 minutes without stirring until the edges begin to set.
4. Transfer the skillet to the preheated oven and bake for 15-20 minutes, or until the frittata is fully set and lightly golden on top.
5. Allow to cool slightly, garnish with fresh herbs, and slice into wedges to serve.

Nutritional Information (per serving):

- *Calories: 210*
- *Protein: 13g*
- *Carbohydrates: 6g*
- *Fats: 15g*
- *Fiber: 1g*
- *Cholesterol: 380mg*
- *Sodium: 290mg*
- *Potassium: 300mg*

Spanish Tortilla with Potatoes and Onions

Yield: 6 servings
Preparation Time: 15 minutes
Cooking Time: 30 minutes

Ingredients:

- 4 medium potatoes, peeled and thinly sliced (about 2 cups)
- 1 medium onion, thinly sliced
- 6 large eggs
- 1/4 cup olive oil
- Salt and pepper to taste
- Fresh parsley (optional, for garnish)

Instructions:

1. Heat olive oil in a large skillet over medium heat, then add the sliced potatoes and onions; cook for about 15 minutes, stirring occasionally, until tender.
2. In a bowl, whisk the eggs and season with salt and pepper, then drain the potatoes and onions and mix them into the egg mixture.
3. Wipe out the skillet, add a little more olive oil, and return to medium heat; pour in the egg and potato mixture, spreading evenly.
4. Cook for 5 minutes, then cover the skillet and cook for an additional 10-15 minutes, or until the eggs are set; gently flip the tortilla using a plate if necessary.
5. Once cooked, let it cool slightly, slice into wedges, and garnish with fresh parsley before serving.

Nutritional Information (per serving):

- *Calories: 220*
- *Protein: 8g*
- *Carbohydrates: 25g*
- *Fats: 10g*
- *Fiber: 2g*
- *Cholesterol: 210mg*
- *Sodium: 250mg*
- *Potassium: 470mg*

Fig and Walnut Oatmeal

Yield: 2 servings
Preparation Time: 5 minutes
Cooking Time: 10 minutes

Ingredients:

- 1 cup rolled oats
- 2 cups water or milk (dairy or plant-based)
- 1/2 cup fresh or dried figs, chopped
- 1/4 cup walnuts, chopped
- 1 tablespoon honey or maple syrup (optional)
- 1/2 teaspoon cinnamon (optional)
- Pinch of salt
- Fresh mint leaves (optional, for garnish)

Instructions:

1. In a medium saucepan, bring water or milk to a boil, then add rolled oats and a pinch of salt; reduce heat and simmer for about 5 minutes, stirring occasionally.
2. Add chopped figs, walnuts, and cinnamon (if using) to the oatmeal; cook for an additional 2-3 minutes until creamy and the figs are softened.
3. Remove from heat and stir in honey or maple syrup if desired.
4. Divide the oatmeal into bowls and garnish with additional figs, walnuts, and fresh mint leaves.
5. Serve warm and enjoy the nutritious benefits of this Mediterranean-inspired breakfast.

Nutritional Information (per serving):

- *Calories: 280*
- *Protein: 8g*
- *Carbohydrates: 50g*
- *Fats: 10g*
- *Fiber: 7g*
- *Cholesterol: 0mg*
- *Sodium: 20mg*
- *Potassium: 450mg*

Tomato and Olive Breakfast Bruschetta

Yield: *4 servings*
Preparation Time: *10 minutes*
Cooking Time: *5 minutes*

Ingredients:
- 1 baguette or ciabatta loaf, sliced into 1/2-inch thick pieces (8-10 slices)
- 2 cups ripe tomatoes, diced
- 1/2 cup black or green olives, pitted and chopped
- 2 tablespoons extra virgin olive oil
- 1 tablespoon balsamic vinegar (optional)
- 2 cloves garlic, minced
- 1/4 cup fresh basil, chopped (or 1 teaspoon dried basil)
- Salt and pepper to taste
- Optional toppings: feta cheese, red pepper flakes

Instructions:
1. Preheat the oven to 400°F (200°C). Arrange the bread slices on a baking sheet and drizzle with olive oil; bake for about 5 minutes until lightly toasted.
2. In a mixing bowl, combine diced tomatoes, chopped olives, minced garlic, olive oil, balsamic vinegar (if using), and basil; season with salt and pepper.
3. Remove the toasted bread from the oven and let it cool slightly.
4. Spoon the tomato and olive mixture onto each toasted slice of bread.
5. Serve immediately, garnished with feta cheese and red pepper flakes if desired.

Nutritional Information (per serving):
- **Calories:** *180*
- **Protein:** *5g*
- **Carbohydrates:** *24g*
- **Fats:** *8g*
- **Fiber:** *2g*
- **Cholesterol:** *0mg*
- **Sodium:** *250mg*
- **Potassium:** *200mg*

Baked Eggs with Spinach and Tomatoes

Yield: *4 servings*
Preparation Time: *10 minutes*
Cooking Time: *20 minutes*

Ingredients:
- 4 large eggs
- 2 cups fresh spinach, chopped
- 1 cup cherry tomatoes, halved
- 2 tablespoons extra virgin olive oil
- 1/2 teaspoon garlic powder
- 1/2 teaspoon salt
- 1/4 teaspoon black pepper
- 1/4 teaspoon red pepper flakes (optional)
- 1/4 cup feta cheese, crumbled (optional)
- Fresh herbs for garnish (such as basil or parsley)

Instructions:
1. Preheat the oven to 375°F (190°C) and grease a baking dish with olive oil.
2. In the baking dish, layer the chopped spinach and halved cherry tomatoes; drizzle with olive oil and sprinkle with garlic powder, salt, pepper, and red pepper flakes.
3. Make four small wells in the vegetables and crack an egg into each well; sprinkle with feta cheese if desired.
4. Bake for 15-20 minutes or until the egg whites are set and the yolks are cooked to your liking.
5. Garnish with fresh herbs and serve warm with whole-grain bread or pita for a complete meal.

Nutritional Information (per serving):
- **Calories:** *180*
- **Protein:** *12g*
- **Carbohydrates:** *6g*
- **Fats:** *13g*
- **Fiber:** *2g*
- **Cholesterol:** *370mg*
- **Sodium:** *400mg*
- **Potassium:** *380mg*

Almond and Orange Scones

Yield: *8 scones*
Preparation Time: *15 minutes*
Cooking Time: *20 minutes*

Ingredients:

- 1 ¾ cups whole wheat flour
- 1/2 cup almond flour
- 1/4 cup sugar (or honey for a healthier option)
- 1 tablespoon baking powder
- 1/2 teaspoon salt
- 1/4 cup cold unsalted butter, cubed (or coconut oil for a dairy-free option)
- 1/2 cup Greek yogurt (or plant-based yogurt)
- Zest of 1 orange
- 1/4 cup fresh orange juice
- 1/2 cup slivered almonds (optional)
- 1 teaspoon almond extract (optional)

Instructions:

1. Preheat the oven to 400°F (200°C) and line a baking sheet with parchment paper.
2. In a large bowl, whisk together whole wheat flour, almond flour, sugar, baking powder, and salt; cut in the butter until the mixture resembles coarse crumbs.
3. Stir in the Greek yogurt, orange zest, orange juice, and almond extract until just combined; fold in slivered almonds if using.
4. Turn the dough onto a floured surface, gently knead it a few times, and shape it into a circle about 1 inch thick; cut into 8 wedges and place on the prepared baking sheet.
5. Bake for 20 minutes or until golden brown; serve warm, optionally with a drizzle of honey or a dollop of yogurt.

Nutritional Information (per scone):

- *Calories:* *170*
- *Protein:* *5g*
- *Carbohydrates:* *23g*
- *Fats:* *7g*
- *Fiber:* *3g*
- *Cholesterol:* *15mg*
- *Sodium:* *150mg*
- *Potassium:* *130mg*

CHAPTER 3: SNACKS AND APPETIZERS

Tzatziki with Fresh Cucumbers and Dill

Yield: 6 servings
Preparation Time: 10 minutes
Cooking Time: 0 minutes

Ingredients:

- 1 1/2 cups plain Greek yogurt
- 1 cucumber, grated and drained
- 2 garlic cloves, minced
- 1 tbsp fresh dill, chopped
- 1 tbsp fresh lemon juice
- 1 tbsp olive oil
- Salt and pepper to taste

Instructions:

1. Grate the cucumber, then place it in a clean towel or sieve to squeeze out excess water.
2. In a bowl, combine the Greek yogurt, grated cucumber, minced garlic, dill, lemon juice, and olive oil.
3. Season with salt and pepper to taste, stirring everything until well-mixed.
4. Chill the tzatziki in the refrigerator for at least 30 minutes to let the flavors meld.
5. Serve cold with pita bread, grilled meats, or as a dip for vegetables.

Nutritional Information (per serving):

- *Calories: 70*
- *Protein: 4g*
- *Carbohydrates: 4g*
- *Fats: 4g*
- *Fiber: 0.5g*
- *Cholesterol: 5mg*
- *Sodium: 90mg*
- *Potassium: 160mg*

Goat Cheese Stuffed Peppadews

Yield: 4 servings
Preparation Time: 10 minutes
Cooking Time: 0 minutes

Ingredients:

- 20 peppadew peppers (jarred, drained)
- 4 oz goat cheese
- 1 tbsp fresh parsley, chopped
- 1 tbsp olive oil
- 1/2 tsp lemon zest
- Salt and pepper to taste

Instructions:

1. In a small bowl, mix the goat cheese, parsley, lemon zest, olive oil, salt, and pepper until smooth.
2. Spoon or pipe the goat cheese mixture into each peppadew pepper, filling them completely.
3. Arrange the stuffed peppadews on a serving platter.
4. Drizzle with a bit more olive oil and garnish with extra parsley or lemon zest if desired.
5. Serve immediately as an appetizer or part of a Mediterranean antipasto platter.

Nutritional Information (per serving):

- *Calories: 120*
- *Protein: 5g*
- *Carbohydrates: 6g*
- *Fats: 9g*
- *Fiber: 1g*
- *Cholesterol: 10mg*
- *Sodium: 240mg*
- *Potassium: 100mg*

Tzatziki with Fresh Cucumbers and Dill

Yield: 6 servings
Preparation Time: 10 minutes
Cooking Time: 0 minutes

Ingredients:

- 1 1/2 cups plain Greek yogurt
- 1 cucumber, grated and drained
- 2 garlic cloves, minced
- 1 tbsp fresh dill, chopped
- 1 tbsp fresh lemon juice
- 1 tbsp olive oil
- Salt and pepper to taste

Instructions:

6. Grate the cucumber, then place it in a clean towel or sieve to squeeze out excess water.
7. In a bowl, combine the Greek yogurt, grated cucumber, minced garlic, dill, lemon juice, and olive oil.
8. Season with salt and pepper to taste, stirring everything until well-mixed.
9. Chill the tzatziki in the refrigerator for at least 30 minutes to let the flavors meld.
10. Serve cold with pita bread, grilled meats, or as a dip for vegetables.

Nutritional Information (per serving):

- *Calories: 70*
- *Protein: 4g*
- *Carbohydrates: 4g*
- *Fats: 4g*
- *Fiber: 0.5g*
- *Cholesterol: 5mg*
- *Sodium: 90mg*
- *Potassium: 160mg*

Goat Cheese Stuffed Peppadews

Yield: 4 servings
Preparation Time: 10 minutes
Cooking Time: 0 minutes

Ingredients:

- 20 peppadew peppers (jarred, drained)
- 4 oz goat cheese
- 1 tbsp fresh parsley, chopped
- 1 tbsp olive oil
- 1/2 tsp lemon zest
- Salt and pepper to taste

Instructions:

6. In a small bowl, mix the goat cheese, parsley, lemon zest, olive oil, salt, and pepper until smooth.
7. Spoon or pipe the goat cheese mixture into each peppadew pepper, filling them completely.
8. Arrange the stuffed peppadews on a serving platter.
9. Drizzle with a bit more olive oil and garnish with extra parsley or lemon zest if desired.
10. Serve immediately as an appetizer or part of a Mediterranean antipasto platter.

Nutritional Information (per serving):

- *Calories: 120*
- *Protein: 5g*
- *Carbohydrates: 6g*
- *Fats: 9g*
- *Fiber: 1g*
- *Cholesterol: 10mg*
- *Sodium: 240mg*
- *Potassium: 100m*

Garlic and Lemon Marinated Olives

Yield: *6 servings*
Preparation Time: *10 minutes*
Cooking Time: *0 minutes*

Ingredients:

- 2 cups mixed olives (green, Kalamata, or black)
- 3 garlic cloves, thinly sliced
- 1 lemon, zested and juiced
- 1/4 cup extra virgin olive oil
- 1 tsp dried oregano
- 1/2 tsp crushed red pepper flakes (optional)
- Fresh rosemary or thyme sprigs (optional)
- Salt and pepper to taste

Instructions:

1. In a mixing bowl, combine the olives, garlic, lemon zest, lemon juice, olive oil, oregano, red pepper flakes, salt, and pepper.
2. Add fresh rosemary or thyme sprigs for extra flavor, if desired.
3. Stir everything together to evenly coat the olives with the marinade.
4. Cover and refrigerate for at least 2 hours, preferably overnight, to allow the flavors to meld.
5. Serve at room temperature as part of a Mediterranean appetizer platter or with crusty bread.

Nutritional Information (per serving):

- *Calories: 120*
- *Protein: 1g*
- *Carbohydrates: 2g*
- *Fats: 12g*
- *Fiber: 1g*
- *Cholesterol: 0mg*
- *Sodium: 400mg*
- *Potassium: 40mg*

Roasted Red Pepper and Feta Dip

Yield: *4 servings*
Preparation Time: *10 minutes*
Cooking Time: *5 minutes*

Ingredients:

- 2 large roasted red bell peppers, jarred or homemade
- 1/2 cup crumbled feta cheese
- 2 tbsp extra virgin olive oil
- 1 garlic clove, minced
- 1 tsp lemon juice
- 1/2 tsp smoked paprika
- Fresh parsley, for garnish
- Salt and pepper to taste

Instructions:

1. In a food processor, blend roasted red peppers, feta cheese, olive oil, garlic, lemon juice, and smoked paprika until smooth.
2. Taste and season with salt and pepper as needed.
3. Transfer the dip to a bowl and drizzle with a bit of extra olive oil on top.
4. Garnish with chopped parsley and an extra pinch of paprika for color.
5. Serve with whole wheat pita chips, cucumber slices, or carrot sticks.

Nutritional Information (per serving):

- *Calories: 150*
- *Protein: 4g*
- *Carbohydrates: 4g*
- *Fats: 13g*
- *Fiber: 1g*
- *Cholesterol: 16mg*
- *Sodium: 340mg*
- *Potassium: 150mg*

Hummus Trio with Pita Bread

Yield: *6 servings*
Preparation Time: *20 minutes*
Cooking Time: *10 minutes*

Ingredients:

Classic Hummus:

- 1 can (15 oz) chickpeas, drained
- 2 tbsp tahini
- 2 tbsp lemon juice
- 1 garlic clove, minced
- 2 tbsp extra virgin olive oil
- 1/2 tsp ground cumin
- Salt to taste

Roasted Red Pepper Hummus:

- 1/2 cup classic hummus (from above)
- 1/2 roasted red bell pepper
- 1/4 tsp smoked paprika

Herb Hummus:

- 1/2 cup classic hummus (from above)
- 1/4 cup fresh parsley, chopped
- 2 tbsp fresh basil
- 1 tbsp lemon zest

Pita Bread:

- 6 whole wheat pita bread rounds, toasted

Instructions:

1. For the *Classic Hummus*, blend chickpeas, tahini, lemon juice, garlic, olive oil, cumin, and salt in a food processor until smooth. Adjust seasoning if necessary.
2. To make *Roasted Red Pepper Hummus*, blend 1/2 cup of the classic hummus with roasted red pepper and smoked paprika until well combined.
3. For *Herb Hummus*, mix 1/2 cup of the classic hummus with fresh parsley, basil, and lemon zest in a bowl until smooth.
4. Toast the pita bread in the oven or on a skillet for 2-3 minutes per side, until golden and slightly crispy.
5. Serve the hummus trio with warm pita bread, drizzling extra olive oil on top and garnishing with paprika, parsley, or sesame seeds.

Nutritional Information (per serving):

- *Calories:* *275*
- *Protein:* *8g*
- *Carbohydrates:* *33g*
- *Fats:* *12g*
- *Fiber:* *8g*
- *Cholesterol:* *0mg*
- *Sodium:* *400mg*
- *Potassium:* *300mg*

Greek Spanakopita Triangles

Yield: 12 triangles (6 servings)
Preparation Time: 20 minutes
Cooking Time: 25 minutes

Ingredients:

- 1 lb (450g) fresh spinach, chopped
- 1/2 cup crumbled feta cheese
- 1/4 cup ricotta cheese
- 1 small onion, finely chopped
- 2 garlic cloves, minced
- 2 tbsp olive oil
- 1 tbsp fresh dill, chopped (optional)
- 1 large egg, beaten
- 1/4 tsp nutmeg
- Salt and pepper to taste
- 12 sheets of phyllo dough, thawed
- Olive oil for brushing

Instructions:

1. Preheat the oven to 375°F (190°C). Sauté the chopped onion and garlic in 2 tbsp of olive oil until soft, then add spinach and cook until wilted. Let it cool slightly.
2. In a bowl, combine the cooked spinach, feta, ricotta, egg, dill, nutmeg, salt, and pepper.
3. Cut the phyllo sheets into strips (about 3 inches wide). Brush each strip with olive oil, place a spoonful of the spinach mixture on one end, and fold the strip into triangles.
4. Place the triangles on a baking sheet and bake for 20-25 minutes, or until golden and crispy.
5. Serve warm, garnished with extra fresh dill or lemon wedges.

Nutritional Information (per serving):

- *Calories: 180*
- *Protein: 6g*
- *Carbohydrates: 14g*
- *Fats: 11g*
- *Fiber: 2g*
- *Cholesterol: 40mg*
- *Sodium: 300mg*
- *Potassium: 300mg*

Mediterranean Stuffed Grape Leaves (Dolma)

Yield: 6 servings (about 24 dolmas)
Preparation Time: 30 minutes
Cooking Time: 45 minutes

Ingredients:

- 1 jar (16 oz) grape leaves, rinsed and drained
- 1 cup uncooked short-grain rice
- 1 small onion, finely chopped
- 1/4 cup fresh parsley, chopped
- 1/4 cup fresh dill, chopped
- 1/4 cup pine nuts (optional)
- 1/4 cup raisins (optional)
- 1/4 cup olive oil, divided
- 2 tbsp lemon juice
- 2 cups vegetable broth
- Salt and pepper to taste

Instructions:

1. Sauté the chopped onion in 2 tbsp olive oil until soft. Add the rice, parsley, dill, pine nuts, raisins, salt, and pepper, cooking for a few minutes until the rice is lightly toasted. Remove from heat and let the filling cool.
2. Place a grape leaf on a flat surface, vein-side up. Add 1 tablespoon of the rice mixture to the center, fold in the sides, and roll tightly into a small log.
3. Layer the stuffed grape leaves seam-side down in a large pot, drizzle with the remaining olive oil, lemon juice, and pour the vegetable broth over.
4. Cover the pot and simmer on low heat for 45 minutes, until the rice is fully cooked and the grape leaves are tender.
5. Serve warm or chilled, garnished with lemon wedges and a drizzle of olive oil.

Nutritional Information (per serving):
- *Calories: 180*
- *Protein: 3g*
- *Carbohydrates: 20g*
- *Fats: 9g*
- *Fiber: 2g*
- *Cholesterol: 0mg*
- *Sodium: 300mg*
- *Potassium: 180mg*

Crispy Falafel with Tahini Sauce

Yield: 4 servings
Preparation Time: 15 minutes (plus 1 hour chilling time)
Cooking Time: 15 minutes

Ingredients:

For the Falafel:

- 1 1/2 cups dried chickpeas, soaked overnight
- 1 small onion, finely chopped
- 3 garlic cloves, minced
- 1/4 cup fresh parsley, chopped
- 1/4 cup fresh cilantro, chopped
- 1 tsp cumin
- 1 tsp coriander
- 1/2 tsp baking powder
- Salt and pepper to taste
- Olive oil for frying

For the Tahini Sauce:

- 1/4 cup tahini
- 2 tbsp lemon juice
- 2 tbsp water
- 1 garlic clove, minced
- Salt to taste

Instructions:

1. Drain the soaked chickpeas and pulse in a food processor with onion, garlic, parsley, cilantro, cumin, coriander, baking powder, salt, and pepper until the mixture holds together. Chill for 1 hour.
2. Shape the falafel mixture into small balls or patties. Heat olive oil in a skillet and fry the falafel in batches for 3-4 minutes per side until golden and crispy.
3. For the tahini sauce, whisk together tahini, lemon juice, water, garlic, and salt until smooth.
4. Serve the falafel with the tahini sauce on the side, along with fresh vegetables or pita.
5. Garnish with additional parsley or cilantro for extra flavor and freshness.

Nutritional Information (per serving):

- **Calories:** *350*
- **Protein:** *12g*
- **Carbohydrates:** *35g*
- **Fats:** *20g*
- **Fiber:** *8g*
- **Cholesterol:** *0mg*
- **Sodium:** *300mg*
- **Potassium:** *500mg*

Grilled Halloumi with Mint and Lemon

Yield: 4 servings
Preparation Time: 10 minutes
Cooking Time: 6 minutes

Ingredients:

- 8 oz halloumi cheese, sliced into 1/2-inch thick pieces
- 2 tbsp olive oil
- 2 tbsp fresh mint, chopped
- Juice and zest of 1 lemon
- Salt and pepper to taste

Instructions:
1. Preheat a grill or grill pan over medium heat and brush the halloumi slices with olive oil on both sides.
2. Grill the halloumi for 2-3 minutes on each side until golden brown and slightly crispy.
3. In a small bowl, combine the lemon juice, lemon zest, chopped mint, salt, and pepper to create a dressing.
4. Once grilled, place the halloumi on serving platter and drizzle with the lemon mint dressing.
5. Serve warm as an appetizer or side dish garnished with additional mint if desired.

Nutritional Information (per serving):
- **Calories:** *250*
- **Protein:** *12g*
- **Carbohydrates:** *2g*
- **Fats:** *22g*
- **Fiber:** *0g*
- **Cholesterol:** *50mg*
- **Sodium:** *700mg*
- **Potassium:** *150mg*

Muhammara (Roasted Red Pepper and Walnut Dip)

Yield: 6 servings
Preparation Time: 15 minutes
Cooking Time: 15 minutes

Ingredients:

- 1 cup walnuts, toasted
- 1 cup roasted red peppers (jarred or homemade)
- 2 cloves garlic, minced
- 1 tbsp pomegranate molasses (or more to taste)
- 2 tbsp olive oil
- 1/2 tsp cumin
- 1/4 tsp red pepper flakes (optional)
- Salt to taste
- Fresh parsley, for garnish (optional)

Instructions:

1. In a food processor, combine the toasted walnuts, roasted red peppers, minced garlic, pomegranate molasses, olive oil, cumin, red pepper flakes, and salt.
2. Blend until smooth, scraping down the sides as needed; add water if you prefer a thinner consistency.
3. Taste and adjust seasoning, adding more pomegranate molasses for sweetness or salt as needed.
4. Transfer the dip to a serving bowl and drizzle with olive oil and sprinkle with fresh parsley if desired.
5. Serve with pita bread, fresh vegetables, or as part of a mezze platter.

Nutritional Information (per serving):

- *Calories: 160*
- *Protein: 4g*
- *Carbohydrates: 8g*
- *Fats: 14g*
- *Fiber: 2g*
- *Cholesterol: 0mg*
- *Sodium: 80mg*
- *Potassium: 150mg*

Bruschetta with Tomato, Basil, and Balsamic

Yield: 6 servings
Preparation Time: 10 minutes
Cooking Time: 5 minutes

Ingredients:

- 1 French baguette or Italian ciabatta, sliced into 1/2-inch pieces
- 2 cups ripe tomatoes, diced (Roma or heirloom work well)
- 1/4 cup fresh basil leaves, chopped
- 2 cloves garlic, minced
- 2 tbsp balsamic vinegar
- 2 tbsp extra virgin olive oil
- Salt and pepper to taste
- Optional: 1/4 cup grated Parmesan cheese or crumbled feta for topping

Instructions:

1. Preheat the oven to 400°F (200°C) and arrange the baguette slices on a baking sheet; drizzle with olive oil and toast for about 5 minutes until golden.
2. In a bowl, combine diced tomatoes, chopped basil, minced garlic, balsamic vinegar, olive oil, salt, and pepper; mix well.
3. Spoon the tomato mixture onto the toasted baguette slices, ensuring even distribution.
4. If desired, sprinkle grated Parmesan or crumbled feta cheese over the top for added flavor.
5. Serve immediately as an appetizer or snack, drizzled with additional balsamic glaze if desired.

Nutritional Information (per serving):

- *Calories: 120*
- *Protein: 4g*
- *Carbohydrates: 17g*
- *Fats: 5g*
- *Fiber: 1g*
- *Cholesterol: 2mg*
- *Sodium: 150mg*
- *Potassium: 220mg*

Baba Ganoush with Smoky Eggplant

Yield: 6 servings
Preparation Time: 10 minutes
Cooking Time: 30 minutes

Ingredients:

- 2 medium eggplants (about 1 pound total)
- 3 tbsp tahini
- 2 tbsp extra virgin olive oil
- 2 cloves garlic, minced
- 2 tbsp lemon juice (freshly squeezed)
- 1/2 tsp smoked paprika (or more to taste)
- Salt to taste
- Fresh parsley, for garnish (optional)
- Pita bread or veggie sticks for serving

Instructions:

1. Preheat the oven to 400°F (200°C). Prick the eggplants several times with a fork and place them on a baking sheet; roast for about 30 minutes until the skin is charred and the flesh is tender.
2. Once cooled, scoop the flesh out of the eggplants and place it in a food processor along with tahini, olive oil, garlic, lemon juice, smoked paprika, and salt.
3. Blend until smooth, adjusting the seasoning as needed, and add a splash of water for a creamier texture if desired.
4. Transfer the baba ganoush to a serving bowl, drizzle with additional olive oil, and garnish with fresh parsley if desired.
5. Serve with pita bread or vegetable sticks for dipping.

Nutritional Information (per serving):

- *Calories: 100*
- *Protein: 3g*
- *Carbohydrates: 8g*
- *Fats: 7g*
- *Fiber: 3g*
- *Cholesterol: 0mg*
- *Sodium: 80mg*
- *Potassium: 200mg*

Zucchini Fritters with Dill and Feta

Yield: 4 servings
Preparation Time: 15 minutes
Cooking Time: 20 minutes

Ingredients:

- 2 medium zucchinis, grated (about 2 cups)
- 1/2 teaspoon salt
- 1/2 cup feta cheese, crumbled
- 1/4 cup fresh dill, chopped (or 1 tablespoon dried dill)
- 1/2 cup breadcrumbs (whole wheat preferred)
- 2 large eggs, beaten
- 1/4 cup green onions or chives, finely chopped
- 1/4 teaspoon black pepper
- Olive oil, for frying

Instructions:
1. In a bowl, combine grated zucchini and salt; let it sit for 10 minutes to release excess moisture, then drain and squeeze out any remaining liquid.
2. In a mixing bowl, combine the drained zucchini, feta, dill, breadcrumbs, beaten eggs, green onions, and black pepper; mix until well combined.
3. Heat olive oil in a skillet over medium heat; scoop about 2 tablespoons of the mixture for each fritter and flatten slightly in the skillet.
4. Cook for 3-4 minutes on each side or until golden brown and crispy; transfer to paper towel-lined plate to drain excess oil.
5. Serve warm, garnished with additional dill or yogurt sauce, and enjoy as a light meal or appetizer.

Nutritional Information (per serving):
- *Calories: 160*
- *Protein: 7g*
- *Carbohydrates: 14g*
- *Fats: 9g*
- *Fiber: 2g*
- *Cholesterol: 100mg*
- *Sodium: 400mg*
- *Potassium: 250mg*

Greek Meatballs (Keftedes) with Lemon Yogurt Dip

Yield: 4 servings
Preparation Time: 15 minute
Cooking Time: 20 minutes

Ingredients:
For the Meatballs:
- 1 pound ground lean lamb or beef
- 1/2 cup breadcrumbs (whole wheat preferred)
- 1/4 cup fresh parsley, finely chopped
- 1/4 cup onion, finely chopped
- 2 cloves garlic, minced
- 1 tsp dried oregano
- 1/2 tsp ground cumin
- 1/2 tsp salt
- 1/4 tsp black pepper
- 1 egg, beaten

For the Lemon Yogurt Dip:
- 1 cup plain Greek yogurt
- 1 tbsp lemon juice (freshly squeezed)
- 1 tsp lemon zest
- 1 tbsp fresh dill or parsley, chopped (optional)
- Salt and pepper, to taste

Instructions:
1. In a large bowl, combine the ground meat, breadcrumbs, parsley, onion, garlic, oregano, cumin, salt, pepper, and beaten egg; mix well and form into small meatballs.
2. Heat a skillet over medium heat with a little olive oil; cook the meatballs for about 10-15 minutes, turning occasionally, until browned and cooked through.
3. For the dip, whisk together the Greek yogurt, lemon juice, lemon zest, dill (if using), salt, and pepper in a separate bowl until smooth.
4. Serve the meatballs warm, accompanied by the lemon yogurt dip on the side.
5. Garnish with additional herbs if desired, and enjoy as an appetizer or main dish with a side of fresh veggies or a Greek salad.

Nutritional Information (per serving):
- *Calories: 250*
- *Protein: 22g*
- *Carbohydrates: 18g*
- *Fats: 12g*
- *Fiber: 1g*
- *Cholesterol: 65mg*
- *Sodium: 350mg*
- *Potassium: 300m*

Chickpea and Parsley Patties

Yield: 4 servings
Preparation Time: 15 minutes
Cooking Time: 20 minutes

Ingredients:
- 1 can (15 oz) chickpeas, drained and rinsed
- 1 cup fresh parsley, chopped
- 1/2 small onion, finely chopped
- 2 cloves garlic, minced
- 1/2 cup breadcrumbs (whole wheat for a healthier option)
- 1 egg (or 1 flax egg for a vegan option)
- 1 teaspoon ground cumin
- 1 teaspoon lemon juice
- Salt and pepper to taste
- Olive oil for frying

Instructions:
1. In a large bowl, mash the chickpeas with a fork or potato masher until mostly smooth, then mix in the chopped parsley, onion, garlic, breadcrumbs, egg, cumin, lemon juice, salt, and pepper.
2. Shape the mixture into small patties (about 2-3 inches in diameter).
3. Heat olive oil in a skillet over medium heat and cook the patties for 4-5 minutes on each side until golden brown and crispy.
4. Remove from the skillet and let drain on paper towels.
5. Serve warm with a yogurt or tahini sauce and a side of fresh salad or in pita bread.

Nutritional Information (per serving):
- *Calories: 180*
- *Protein: 7g*
- *Carbohydrates: 24g*
- *Fats: 7g*
- *Fiber: 6g*
- *Cholesterol: 40mg (if using egg)*
- *Sodium: 250mg*
- *Potassium: 300mg*

Roasted Red Pepper and Feta Dip

Yield: 4 servings
Preparation Time: 10 minutes
Cooking Time: 5 minutes

Ingredients:

- 2 large roasted red bell peppers, jarred or homemade
- 1/2 cup crumbled feta cheese
- 2 tbsp extra virgin olive oil
- 1 garlic clove, minced
- 1 tsp lemon juice
- 1/2 tsp smoked paprika
- Fresh parsley, for garnish
- Salt and pepper to taste

Instructions:

6. In a food processor, blend roasted red peppers, feta cheese, olive oil, garlic, lemon juice, and smoked paprika until smooth.
7. Taste and season with salt and pepper as needed.
8. Transfer the dip to a bowl and drizzle with a bit of extra olive oil on top.
9. Garnish with chopped parsley and an extra pinch of paprika for color.
10. Serve with whole wheat pita chips, cucumber slices, or carrot sticks.

Nutritional Information (per serving):

- *Calories: 150*
- *Protein: 4g*
- *Carbohydrates: 4g*
- *Fats: 13g*
- *Fiber: 1g*
- *Cholesterol: 16mg*
- *Sodium: 340mg*
- *Potassium: 150mg*

Roasted Garlic White Bean Dip

Yield: 6 servings
Preparation Time: 10 minutes
Cooking Time: 30 minutes

Ingredients:

- 1 head of garlic
- 1 can (15 oz) white beans (cannellini or navy), drained and rinsed
- 2 tablespoons olive oil, plus more for drizzling
- 2 tablespoons lemon juice
- 1 teaspoon ground cumin
- 1/2 teaspoon salt
- 1/4 teaspoon black pepper
- Fresh herbs for garnish (e.g., parsley or thyme)
- Optional: red pepper flakes for a spicy kick

Instructions:

1. Preheat the oven to 400°F (200°C). Cut the top off the garlic head, drizzle with olive oil, wrap in foil, and roast for 30 minutes until soft.
2. In a food processor, combine the white beans, roasted garlic (squeezed out of the skins), 2 tablespoons olive oil, lemon juice, cumin, salt, and black pepper; blend until smooth.
3. Adjust the consistency with water if necessary, blending until creamy.
4. Taste and adjust seasoning; add red pepper flakes if desired.
5. Serve the dip drizzled with olive oil and garnished with fresh herbs, alongside pita chips or fresh veggies.

Nutritional Information (per serving):

- *Calories: 110*
- *Protein: 5g*
- *Carbohydrates: 15g*
- *Fats: 4g*
- *Fiber: 4g*
- *Cholesterol: 0mg*
- *Sodium: 250mg*
- *Potassium: 250mg*

CHAPTER 4: SALAD RECIPES

Classic Greek Salad with Feta and Olives

Yield: *4 servings*
Preparation Time: *15 minutes*
Cooking Time: *0 minutes*

Ingredients:
- 2 cups cucumbers, diced
- 2 cups cherry tomatoes, halved
- 1 cup red bell pepper, diced
- 1/2 cup red onion, thinly sliced
- 1 cup Kalamata olives, pitted
- 1 cup feta cheese, crumbled
- 1/4 cup extra virgin olive oil
- 2 tablespoons red wine vinegar
- 1 teaspoon dried oregano
- Salt and pepper to taste
- Fresh parsley for garnish (optional)

Instructions:
1. In a large salad bowl, combine the diced cucumbers, halved cherry tomatoes, diced bell pepper, sliced red onion, and Kalamata olives.
2. In a separate small bowl, whisk together the olive oil, red wine vinegar, dried oregano, salt, and pepper to make the dressing.
3. Pour the dressing over the salad and toss gently to combine all ingredients evenly.
4. Sprinkle the crumbled feta cheese on top of the salad and garnish with fresh parsley if desired.
5. Serve immediately as a refreshing side dish or light main course, perfect for any
6. Mediterranean meal.

Nutritional Information (per serving):
- *Calories: 200*
- *Protein: 6g*
- *Carbohydrates: 8g*
- *Fats: 18g*
- *Fiber: 2g*
- *Cholesterol: 30mg*
- *Sodium: 500mg*
- *Potassium: 400mg*

Tabouleh with Fresh Mint and Lemon

Yield: *4 servings*
Preparation Time: *20 minutes*
Cooking Time: *0 minutes*

Ingredients:
- 1/2 cup bulgur wheat
- 1 cup boiling water
- 1 cup fresh parsley, finely chopped
- 1/2 cup fresh mint, finely chopped
- 1 cup tomatoes, diced
- 1/2 cucumber, diced
- 1/4 cup green onions, sliced
- 1/4 cup extra virgin olive oil
- 1/4 cup fresh lemon juice (about 2 lemons)
- Salt and pepper to taste

Instructions:
1. In a bowl, combine bulgur wheat and boiling water, cover, and let it sit for about 15 minutes until the bulgur absorbs the water and is tender.
2. Fluff the bulgur with a fork and let it cool slightly, then transfer it to a large mixing bowl.
3. Add the chopped parsley, mint, diced tomatoes, cucumber, and green onions to the bulgur, mixing well to combine.
4. In a small bowl, whisk together the olive oil, lemon juice, salt, and pepper, then pour over the salad and toss to coat evenly.
5. Serve chilled or at room temperature as a refreshing side dish or light main course, perfect for warm weather meals.

Nutritional Information (per serving):
- *Calories: 180*
- *Protein: 4g*
- *Carbohydrates: 22g*
- *Fats: 8g*
- *Fiber: 5g*
- *Cholesterol: 0mg*
- *Sodium: 40mg*
- *Potassium: 320m g*

Chickpea Salad with Cucumber and Red Onion

Yield: 4 servings
Preparation Time: 15 minutes
Cooking Time: 0 minutes

Ingredients:

- 1 can (15 oz) chickpeas, drained and rinsed
- 1 medium cucumber, diced
- 1/2 red onion, finely chopped
- 1 cup cherry tomatoes, halved
- 1/4 cup fresh parsley, chopped
- 1/4 cup extra virgin olive oil
- 2 tablespoons red wine vinegar
- Juice of 1 lemon
- Salt and pepper to taste
- Optional: 1/2 teaspoon cumin or smoked paprika for added flavor

Instructions:

1. In a large mixing bowl, combine the chickpeas, diced cucumber, red onion, cherry tomatoes, and parsley.
2. In a separate small bowl, whisk together the olive oil, red wine vinegar, lemon juice, salt, and pepper (and cumin or paprika if using).
3. Pour the dressing over the salad and toss gently to combine all the ingredients evenly.
4. Let the salad sit for about 5-10 minutes to allow the flavors to meld.
5. Serve chilled or at room temperature as a nutritious side dish or light meal.

Nutritional Information (per serving):

- *Calories: 210*
- *Protein: 7g*
- *Carbohydrates: 25g*
- *Fats: 10g*
- *Fiber: 6g*
- *Cholesterol: 0mg*
- *Sodium: 300mg*
- *Potassium: 450mg*

Roasted Beet Salad with Goat Cheese

Yield: 4 servings
Preparation Time: 15 minutes
Cooking Time: 45 minutes

Ingredients:

- 4 medium beets, scrubbed and trimmed
- 4 cups mixed salad greens (e.g., arugula, spinach, and romaine)
- 1/2 cup goat cheese, crumbled
- 1/4 cup walnuts, toasted
- 1/4 cup extra virgin olive oil
- 2 tablespoons balsamic vinegar
- Salt and pepper to taste
- Optional: 1 tablespoon fresh herbs (e.g., thyme or basil) for garnish

Instructions:

1. Preheat the oven to 400°F (200°C). Wrap each beet in aluminum foil and place them on a baking sheet; roast for 45 minutes, or until tender.
2. Once cooled, peel the beets and slice them into wedges.
3. In a large bowl, whisk together the olive oil, balsamic vinegar, salt, and pepper.
4. Add the mixed greens, roasted beet wedges, crumbled goat cheese, and toasted walnuts to the bowl, then gently toss to combine.
5. Serve immediately, garnished with fresh herbs if desired.

Nutritional Information (per serving):

- *Calories: 250*
- *Protein: 6g*
- *Carbohydrates: 24g*
- *Fats: 17g*
- *Fiber: 5g*
- *Cholesterol: 7mg*
- *Sodium: 120mg*
- *Potassium: 600mg*

Grilled Halloumi and Watermelon Salad

Yield: 4 servings
Preparation Time: 10 minutes
Cooking Time: 10 minutes

Ingredients:

- 8 ounces halloumi cheese, sliced into 1/2-inch thick pieces
- 4 cups watermelon, cubed
- 2 cups arugula or mixed salad greens
- 1/4 cup fresh mint leaves, chopped (optional)
- 3 tablespoons extra virgin olive oil
- 2 tablespoons balsamic vinegar
- Salt and pepper to taste
- Optional: 1 tablespoon lemon juice for added tang

Instructions:

1. Preheat a grill or grill pan over medium-high heat. Grill the halloumi slices for 2-3 minutes on each side until golden brown and crispy.
2. In a large bowl, combine the watermelon, arugula, and mint (if using).
3. In a separate small bowl, whisk together the olive oil, balsamic vinegar, salt, pepper, and lemon juice (if desired).
4. Pour the dressing over the watermelon mixture and toss gently to combine.
5. Serve the salad topped with the grilled halloumi slices, drizzling any remaining dressing on top.

Nutritional Information (per serving):

- *Calories:* 220
- *Protein:* 10g
- *Carbohydrates:* 15g
- *Fats:* 15g
- *Fiber:* 1g
- *Cholesterol:* 25mg
- *Sodium:* 450mg
- **Potassium:** 350mg

Moroccan Carrot Salad with Cumin and Coriander

Yield: 4 servings
Preparation Time: 15 minutes
Cooking Time: 0 minutes

Ingredients:

- 4 large carrots, peeled and grated
- 1/4 cup fresh parsley, chopped
- 1/4 cup raisins or dried apricots, chopped
- 1/4 teaspoon ground cumin
- 1/4 teaspoon ground coriander
- 3 tablespoons extra virgin olive oil
- 2 tablespoons lemon juice
- Salt and pepper to taste
- Optional: 1/4 teaspoon paprika or cayenne for extra heat

Instructions:

1. In a large bowl, combine the grated carrots, parsley, and raisins (or dried apricots).
2. In a small bowl, whisk together the olive oil, lemon juice, cumin, coriander, salt, and pepper (add paprika or cayenne if desired).
3. Pour the dressing over the carrot mixture and toss well to combine.
4. Let the salad sit for 10 minutes to allow the flavors to meld.
5. Serve chilled or at room temperature, garnished with additional parsley if desired.

Nutritional Information (per serving):

- *Calories:* 140
- *Protein:* 2g
- *Carbohydrates:* 20g
- *Fats:* 7g
- *Fiber:* 3g
- *Cholesterol:* 0mg
- *Sodium:* 85mg
- *Potassium:* 320mg

Arugula Salad with Lemon and Parmesan

Yield: 4 servings
Preparation Time: 10 minutes
Cooking Time: 0 minutes

Ingredients:

- 4 cups fresh arugula, washed and dried
- 1/4 cup shaved Parmesan cheese
- 1/4 cup cherry tomatoes, halved
- 2 tablespoons extra virgin olive oil
- 1 tablespoon fresh lemon juice
- Salt and pepper to taste
- Optional: 1/4 teaspoon red pepper flakes for heat

Instructions:

1. In a large bowl, combine the arugula, cherry tomatoes, and Parmesan cheese.
2. In a small bowl, whisk together the olive oil, lemon juice, salt, pepper, and red pepper flakes (if using).
3. Drizzle the dressing over the salad and toss gently to combine.
4. Adjust seasoning to taste and let the salad sit for a couple of minutes for the flavors to meld.
5. Serve immediately as a refreshing side dish or light main course.

Nutritional Information (per serving):

- *Calories: 130*
- *Protein: 4g*
- *Carbohydrates: 6g*
- *Fats: 12g*
- *Fiber: 1g*
- *Cholesterol: 4mg*
- *Sodium: 150mg*
- *Potassium: 250mg*

Tomato and Cucumber Salad with Fresh Herbs

Yield: 4 servings
Preparation Time: 10 minutes
Cooking Time: 0 minutes

Ingredients:

- 3 medium ripe tomatoes, diced
- 1 large cucumber, diced
- 1/4 red onion, finely chopped
- 1/4 cup fresh parsley, chopped
- 1/4 cup fresh basil, chopped
- 2 tablespoons extra virgin olive oil
- 1 tablespoon red wine vinegar
- Salt and pepper to taste
- Optional: 1/4 teaspoon dried oregano or a squeeze of fresh lemon juice

Instructions:

1. In a large bowl, combine the diced tomatoes, cucumber, red onion, parsley, and basil.
2. In a small bowl, whisk together the olive oil, red wine vinegar, salt, pepper, and oregano or lemon juice (if using).
3. Drizzle the dressing over the salad and toss gently to coat all the ingredients.
4. Let the salad sit for about 5 minutes to allow the flavors to meld.
5. Serve chilled or at room temperature as refreshing side dish or light lunch.

Nutritional Information (per serving):

- *Calories: 90*
- *Protein: 2g*
- *Carbohydrates: 10g*
- *Fats: 5g*
- *Fiber: 2g*
- *Cholesterol: 0mg*
- *Sodium: 120mg*
- *Potassium: 300mg*

Fennel and Orange Salad with Olives

Yield: *4 servings*
Preparation Time: *15 minutes*
Cooking Time: *0 minutes*

Ingredients:

- 1 large fennel bulb, thinly sliced
- 2 large oranges, peeled and segmented
- 1/2 cup Kalamata olives, pitted and halved
- 1/4 red onion, thinly sliced
- 2 tablespoons extra virgin olive oil
- 1 tablespoon red wine vinegar
- Salt and pepper to taste
- Optional: Fresh parsley or mint for garnish

Instructions:

1. In a large bowl, combine the sliced fennel, orange segments, olives, and red onion.
2. In a small bowl, whisk together the olive oil, red wine vinegar, salt, and pepper.
3. Drizzle the dressing over the salad and gently toss to combine all the ingredients.
4. Let the salad sit for 5 minutes to allow the flavors to meld.
5. Serve garnished with fresh parsley or mint, if desired, as a refreshing side or starter.

Nutritional Information (per serving):

- *Calories: 120*
- *Protein: 2g*
- *Carbohydrates: 12g*
- *Fats: 7g*
- *Fiber: 3g*
- *Cholesterol: 0mg*
- *Sodium: 200mg*
- *Potassium: 280mg*

Spinach and Pomegranate Salad with Walnuts

Yield: *4 servings*
Preparation Time: *15 minutes*
Cooking Time: *0 minutes*

Ingredients:

- 6 cups fresh spinach leaves, washed and dried
- 1 cup pomegranate seeds
- 1/2 cup walnuts, toasted and roughly chopped
- 1/4 red onion, thinly sliced
- 1/4 cup feta cheese, crumbled (optional)
- 3 tablespoons extra virgin olive oil
- 1 tablespoon balsamic vinegar
- Salt and pepper to taste
- Optional: Fresh mint or parsley for garnish

Instructions:

1. In a large bowl, combine the spinach, pomegranate seeds, walnuts, red onion, and feta cheese (if using).
2. In a small bowl, whisk together the olive oil, balsamic vinegar, salt, and pepper.
3. Drizzle the dressing over the salad and gently toss to combine all the ingredients.
4. Allow the salad to sit for 5 minutes to let the flavors meld.
5. Serve garnished with fresh mint or parsley, if desired, as a nutritious and vibrant side or main dish.

Nutritional Information (per serving):

- *Calories: 160*
- *Protein: 4g*
- *Carbohydrates: 12g*
- *Fats: 12g*
- *Fiber: 3g*
- *Cholesterol: 5mg*
- *Sodium: 150mg*
- *Potassium: 300mg*

Lentil Salad with Feta and Mint

Yield: 4 servings
Preparation Time: 15 minutes
Cooking Time: 25 minutes

Ingredients:

- 1 cup dry green or brown lentils
- 2 1/2 cups water or vegetable broth
- 1/2 cup feta cheese, crumbled
- 1/2 cup cherry tomatoes, halved
- 1/4 red onion, finely chopped
- 1/4 cup fresh mint leaves, chopped
- 3 tablespoons extra virgin olive oil
- 2 tablespoons lemon juice
- Salt and pepper to taste
- Optional: 1/4 teaspoon red pepper flakes for heat

Instructions:

1. Rinse the lentils and combine them with water or broth in a saucepan; bring to a boil, then reduce heat and simmer for about 25 minutes until tender.
2. While the lentils cook, prepare the dressing by whisking together olive oil, lemon juice, salt, pepper, and red pepper flakes (if using) in a small bowl.
3. Once the lentils are cooked, drain any excess liquid and let them cool slightly before adding them to a large mixing bowl.
4. Add feta cheese, cherry tomatoes, red onion, and mint to the lentils, then pour the dressing over the mixture and toss gently to combine.
5. Serve immediately or refrigerate for 30 minutes to enhance flavors, making it a delicious and nutritious option for lunch or as a side dish.

Nutritional Information (per serving):
- *Calories: 220*
- *Protein: 10g*
- *Carbohydrates: 27g*
- *Fats: 9g*
- *Fiber: 8g*
- *Cholesterol: 20mg*
- *Sodium: 300mg*
- *Potassium: 400mg*

Couscous Salad with Roasted Vegetables

Yield: 4 servings
Preparation Time: 15 minutes
Cooking Time: 30 minutes

Ingredients:

- 1 cup whole wheat couscous
- 1 1/4 cups vegetable broth or water
- 1 medium zucchini, diced
- 1 red bell pepper, diced
- 1 yellow bell pepper, diced
- 1 red onion, chopped
- 2 tablespoons olive oil
- 1 teaspoon dried oregano
- 1/2 teaspoon salt
- 1/4 teaspoon black pepper
- 1/4 cup fresh parsley, chopped
- Juice of 1 lemon
- Optional: Feta cheese for topping

Instructions:

1. Preheat the oven to 425°F (220°C), tos the zucchini, bell peppers, and red onio with olive oil, oregano, salt, and peppe then spread on a baking sheet and roast fo 20-25 minutes until tender.
2. While the vegetables roast, bring th vegetable broth or water to a boil in saucepan, add the couscous, cover, an remove from heat, letting it sit for minutes.
3. Fluff the couscous with a fork, the combine it in a large bowl with the roaste vegetables, chopped parsley, and lemo juice.
4. Mix well and adjust seasoning to taste; l it cool slightly before serving.
5. Serve warm or at room temperature garnished with crumbled feta cheese desired.

Nutritional Information (per serving):
- *Calories: 220*
- *Protein: 6g*
- *Carbohydrates: 30g*
- *Fats: 9g*
- *Fiber: 5g*
- *Cholesterol: 5mg*
- *Sodium: 250mg*
- *Potassium: 400mg*

Avocado and Tomato Mediterranean Salad

Yield: *4 servings*
Preparation Time: *10 minutes*
Cooking Time: *0 minutes*

Ingredients:

- 2 ripe avocados, diced
- 2 cups cherry tomatoes, halved
- 1/2 red onion, thinly sliced
- 1/2 cucumber, diced
- 1/4 cup Kalamata olives, pitted and sliced
- 1/4 cup fresh parsley, chopped
- 3 tablespoons olive oil
- Juice of 1 lemon
- Salt and pepper to taste
- Optional: Crumbled feta cheese for topping

Instructions:

1. In a large bowl, combine the diced avocados, halved cherry tomatoes, sliced red onion, diced cucumber, olives, and chopped parsley.
2. Drizzle olive oil and lemon juice over the salad, then season with salt and pepper to taste.
3. Gently toss the salad to combine, being careful not to mash the avocados.
4. Let the salad sit for 5 minutes to allow flavors to meld.
5. Serve immediately, garnished with crumbled feta cheese if desired.

Nutritional Information (per serving):

- *Calories: 250*
- *Protein: 3g*
- *Carbohydrates: 14g*
- *Fats: 22g*
- *Fiber: 7g*
- *Cholesterol: 0mg*
- *Sodium: 160mg*
- *Potassium: 600mg*

Roasted Red Pepper and Artichoke Salad

Yield: *4 servings*
Preparation Time: *15 minutes*
Cooking Time: *25 minutes*

Ingredients:

- 2 large red bell peppers
- 1 can (14 oz) artichoke hearts, drained and halved
- 1/4 cup Kalamata olives, pitted and sliced
- 1/4 cup red onion, thinly sliced
- 2 tablespoons fresh basil, chopped (or 1 tablespoon dried basil)
- 3 tablespoons olive oil
- 1 tablespoon balsamic vinegar
- Salt and pepper to taste
- Optional: Crumbled feta cheese for topping

Instructions:

1. Preheat the oven to 425°F (220°C). Place the whole red bell peppers on a baking sheet and roast for 20–25 minutes until the skin is charred and blistered.
2. Once roasted, remove the peppers from the oven and cover them with foil for 10 minutes to steam; then peel the skin off and slice into strips.
3. In a large bowl, combine the roasted red pepper strips, artichoke hearts, olives, red onion, and basil.
4. Drizzle with olive oil and balsamic vinegar, then season with salt and pepper to taste; toss gently to combine.
5. Serve chilled or at room temperature, garnished with crumbled feta cheese if desired.

Nutritional Information (per serving):

- *Calories: 180*
- *Protein: 3g*
- *Carbohydrates: 14g*
- *Fats: 12g*
- *Fiber: 5g*
- *Cholesterol: 0mg*
- *Sodium: 210mg*
- *Potassium: 400mg*

Farro Salad with Sun-Dried Tomatoes

Yield: *4 servings*
Preparation Time: *15 minutes*
Cooking Time: *30 minutes*

Ingredients:

- 1 cup farro
- 1/2 cup sun-dried tomatoes, chopped (in oil, drained)
- 1/2 cup cucumber, diced
- 1/4 cup red onion, finely chopped
- 1/4 cup feta cheese, crumbled
- 1/4 cup fresh parsley, chopped
- 3 tablespoons olive oil
- 2 tablespoons balsamic vinegar
- Salt and pepper to taste
- Optional: 1 teaspoon dried oregano or basil

Instructions:

1. Cook the farro according to package instructions, usually boiling in salted water for about 20–30 minutes until tender; drain and cool slightly.
2. In a large bowl, combine the cooked farro, sun-dried tomatoes, cucumber, red onion, parsley, and feta cheese.
3. In a separate small bowl, whisk together the olive oil, balsamic vinegar, salt, pepper, and optional herbs.
4. Pour the dressing over the farro salad mixture and toss gently to combine.
5. Serve chilled or at room temperature, garnished with additional parsley if desired.

Nutritional Information (per serving):

- *Calories: 220*
- *Protein: 8g*
- *Carbohydrates: 30g*
- *Fats: 9g*
- *Fiber: 5g*
- *Cholesterol: 10mg*
- *Sodium: 180mg*
- *Potassium: 250mg*

Eggplant and Tomato Salad with Fresh Basil

Yield: *4 servings*
Preparation Time: *15 minutes*
Cooking Time: *25 minutes*

Ingredients:

- 1 medium eggplant, diced
- 2 cups cherry tomatoes, halved
- 1/4 cup red onion, finely chopped
- 1/4 cup fresh basil leaves, torn
- 3 tablespoons olive oil
- 1 tablespoon balsamic vinegar
- Salt and pepper to taste
- Optional: 1 clove garlic, minced, or 1 teaspoon dried oregano

Instructions:

1. Preheat the oven to 400°F (200°C) and lir a baking sheet with parchment paper; tos the diced eggplant with 1 tablespoon (olive oil, salt, and pepper, then spread out on the baking sheet and roast for abou 20 minutes until tender and golden.
2. In a large mixing bowl, combine th roasted eggplant, cherry tomatoes, re onion, and torn basil leaves.
3. In a small bowl, whisk together th remaining olive oil, balsamic vinegar, an optional garlic or oregano.
4. Drizzle the dressing over the salad and tos gently to combine all the ingredients.
5. Serve immediately at room temperature (chilled, garnished with additional basil desired.

Nutritional Information (per serving):

- *Calories: 150*
- *Protein: 3g*
- *Carbohydrates: 15g*
- *Fats: 9g*
- *Fiber: 5g*
- *Cholesterol: 0mg*
- *Sodium: 200mg*
- *Potassium: 350mg*

Chopped Mediterranean Kale Salad

eld: 4 servings
eparation Time: 15 minutes
ooking Time: 0 minutes

gredients:

- 4 cups kale, stems removed and chopped
- 1 cup cherry tomatoes, halved
- 1/2 cucumber, diced
- 1/4 cup red onion, finely chopped
- 1/2 cup kalamata olives, pitted and sliced
- 1/3 cup feta cheese, crumbled
- 1/4 cup fresh parsley, chopped
- 3 tablespoons olive oil
- 2 tablespoons lemon juice
- Salt and pepper to taste
- Optional: 1 teaspoon dried oregano or crushed red pepper flakes

structions:

1. In a large bowl, combine the chopped kale, cherry tomatoes, cucumber, red onion, kalamata olives, feta cheese, and parsley.
2. In a small bowl, whisk together the olive oil, lemon juice, salt, pepper, and optional oregano or red pepper flakes.
3. Pour the dressing over the salad and toss well to combine, ensuring the kale is coated.
4. Let the salad sit for about 5 minutes to allow the flavors to meld and the kale to soften slightly.
5. Serve chilled or at room temperature, garnished with extra feta or parsley if desired.

Nutritional Information (per serving):
- *Calories:* 200
- *Protein:* 5g
- *Carbohydrates:* 12g
- *Fats:* 16g
- *Fiber:* 4g
- *Cholesterol:* 10mg
- *Sodium:* 350mg
- *Potassium:* 450mg

CHAPTER 5: GRAINS, PASTA, AND RICE RECIPES

Greek Lemon Rice with Fresh Herbs

Yield: *4 servings*
Preparation Time: *10 minutes*
Cooking Time: *20 minutes*

Ingredients:
- 1 cup long-grain rice (e.g., basmati or jasmine)
- 2 cups vegetable or chicken broth
- 2 tablespoons olive oil
- Zest and juice of 1 large lemon
- 1/4 cup fresh parsley, chopped
- 1/4 cup fresh dill, chopped
- Salt and pepper to taste
- Optional: 1/4 cup green onions, sliced

Instructions:
1. Rinse the rice under cold water until clear, then drain.
2. In a medium saucepan, heat olive oil over medium heat, add the rice, and sauté for 2-3 minutes until lightly toasted.
3. Pour in the broth, add lemon zest and juice, then bring to a boil; reduce heat, cover, and simmer for 15 minutes until rice is tender and liquid is absorbed.
4. Remove from heat and let sit for 5 minutes; then fluff with a fork and stir in fresh herbs and green onions if using.
5. Season with salt and pepper to taste before serving, and garnish with additional herbs if desired.

Nutritional Information (per serving):
- *Calories: 190*
- *Protein: 4g*
- *Carbohydrates: 28g*
- *Fats: 7g*
- *Fiber: 1g*
- *Cholesterol: 0mg*
- *Sodium: 350mg*
- *Potassium: 150mg*

Orzo with Roasted Vegetables

Yield: *4 servings*
Preparation Time: *15 minutes*
Cooking Time: *30 minutes*

Ingredients:
- 1 cup orzo pasta
- 2 cups mixed vegetables (e.g., bell peppers, zucchini, cherry tomatoes)
- 2 tablespoons olive oil
- 1 teaspoon dried oregano
- 1 teaspoon garlic powder
- Salt and pepper to taste
- 1/4 cup feta cheese, crumbled (optional)
- 1/4 cup fresh basil, chopped (optional)

Instructions:
1. Preheat the oven to 400°F (200°C) and toss the mixed vegetables with olive oil, oregano, garlic powder, salt, and pepper on a baking sheet.
2. Roast the vegetables in the oven for 2 minutes, stirring halfway through until they are tender and slightly caramelized.
3. Meanwhile, cook the orzo according to package instructions in salted boiling water until al dente, then drain.
4. Combine the roasted vegetables with the cooked orzo in a large bowl, adding feta cheese and fresh basil if desired.
5. Toss everything together and serve warm or at room temperature, drizzling with a bit more olive oil if needed.

Nutritional Information (per serving):
- *Calories: 220*
- *Protein: 6g*
- *Carbohydrates: 30g*
- *Fats: 9g*
- *Fiber: 3g*
- *Cholesterol: 10mg (if using feta)*
- *Sodium: 300mg*
- *Potassium: 350mg*

Creamy Spinach and Feta Risotto

Yield: *4 servings*
Preparation Time: *10 minutes*
Cooking Time: *30 minutes*

Ingredients:

- 1 cup Arborio rice
- 4 cups low-sodium vegetable broth
- 1 cup fresh spinach, chopped
- 1/2 cup feta cheese, crumbled
- 1 small onion, finely chopped
- 2 cloves garlic, minced
- 2 tablespoons olive oil
- 1/4 cup white wine (optional)
- Salt and pepper to taste
- 1 tablespoon fresh dill or parsley, chopped (optional)

Instructions:

1. In a medium saucepan, heat the vegetable broth over low heat and keep it warm.
2. In a large skillet, heat olive oil over medium heat; add the chopped onion and garlic, cooking until softened, about 3-4 minutes.
3. Stir in the Arborio rice, cooking for 1-2 minutes until lightly toasted, then add the white wine (if using), and let it absorb.
4. Gradually add the warm broth, one ladle at a time, stirring frequently until the rice absorbs the liquid before adding more, about 20 minutes.
5. Once creamy and al dente, stir in the spinach and feta, seasoning with salt, pepper, and optional herbs before serving warm.

Nutritional Information (per serving):

- **Calories:** *280*
- **Protein:** *10g*
- **Carbohydrates:** *38g*
- **Fats:** *10g*
- **Fiber:** *2g*
- **Cholesterol:** *30mg*
- **Sodium:** *400mg*
- **Potassium:** *450mg*

Moroccan Couscous with Vegetables

Yield: *4 servings*
Preparation Time: *15 minutes*
Cooking Time: *15 minutes*

Ingredients:

- 1 cup couscous
- 1 1/4 cups vegetable broth (or water)
- 1 medium zucchini, diced
- 1 red bell pepper, diced
- 1 medium carrot, diced
- 1/2 cup chickpeas, rinsed and drained
- 1/2 teaspoon ground cumin
- 1/2 teaspoon ground coriander
- 1/2 teaspoon cinnamon
- 1 tablespoon olive oil
- Salt and pepper to taste
- 1/4 cup fresh parsley or cilantro, chopped (optional)

Instructions:

1. In a skillet, heat olive oil over medium heat, adding zucchini, bell pepper, and carrot; sauté for about 5-7 minutes until softened.
2. Stir in the chickpeas, cumin, coriander, and cinnamon, cooking for an additional 2 minutes to blend flavors.
3. In a separate pot, bring the vegetable broth to a boil, then remove from heat and add couscous, covering the pot to let it steam for 5 minutes.
4. Fluff the couscous with a fork, then mix it with the sautéed vegetables and season with salt, pepper, and optional herbs.
5. Serve warm, garnished with additional fresh herbs if desired.

Nutritional Information (per serving):

- **Calories:** *230*
- **Protein:** *7g*
- **Carbohydrates:** *36g*
- **Fats:** *7g*
- **Fiber:** *5g*
- **Cholesterol:** *0mg*
- **Sodium:** *400mg*
- **Potassium:** *450mg*

Mediterranean Quinoa Pilaf

Yield: *4 servings*
Preparation Time: *10 minutes*
Cooking Time: *20 minutes*

Ingredients:

- 1 cup quinoa, rinsed
- 2 cups vegetable broth (or water)
- 1 small onion, finely chopped
- 2 cloves garlic, minced
- 1 medium red bell pepper, diced
- 1 cup cherry tomatoes, halved
- 1/2 cup Kalamata olives, pitted and chopped
- 1/2 teaspoon dried oregano
- 1/2 teaspoon ground cumin
- 1 tablespoon olive oil
- Salt and pepper to taste
- 1/4 cup fresh parsley or basil, chopped (for garnish)

Instructions:

1. In a medium saucepan, heat olive oil over medium heat and sauté onion and garlic for about 3-4 minutes until softened.
2. Add the red bell pepper and sauté for another 3 minutes before stirring in the quinoa, vegetable broth, oregano, and cumin; bring to a boil.
3. Reduce heat to low, cover, and simmer for 15 minutes or until quinoa is fluffy and liquid is absorbed.
4. Stir in the cherry tomatoes and olives, cooking for an additional 2-3 minutes until heated through; season with salt and pepper.
5. Remove from heat, fluff with a fork, and garnish with fresh herbs before serving.

Nutritional Information (per serving):
- *Calories: 220*
- *Protein: 7g*
- *Carbohydrates: 30g*
- *Fats: 9g*
- *Fiber: 4g*
- *Cholesterol: 0mg*
- *Sodium: 320mg*
- *Potassium: 450mg*

Shrimp and Lemon Zucchini Pasta

Yield: *4 servings*
Preparation Time: *10 minutes*
Cooking Time: *15 minutes*

Ingredients:

- 8 ounces whole wheat spaghetti or zucchini noodles
- 1 pound shrimp, peeled and deveined
- 2 medium zucchinis, spiralized or sliced into thin ribbons
- 3 tablespoons olive oil
- 3 cloves garlic, minced
- Juice and zest of 1 lemon
- 1/4 teaspoon red pepper flakes (optional)
- Salt and pepper to taste
- 1/4 cup fresh parsley, chopped (for garnish)
- Grated Parmesan cheese (optional, for serving)

Instructions:

1. Cook the spaghetti according to package instructions; drain and set aside, reserving 1/2 cup of pasta water.
2. In a large skillet, heat olive oil over medium heat and sauté garlic for 1 minute until fragrant; add shrimp, cooking until pink, about 3-4 minutes.
3. Stir in zucchini, lemon juice, zest, and red pepper flakes, cooking for an additional 2-3 minutes until zucchini is tender.
4. Toss the cooked spaghetti with the shrimp and zucchini mixture, adding reserved pasta water as needed to reach desired consistency; season with salt and pepper.
5. Serve immediately, garnished with fresh parsley and grated Parmesan, if desired.

Nutritional Information (per serving):
- *Calories: 350*
- *Protein: 28g*
- *Carbohydrates: 40g*
- *Fats: 12g*
- *Fiber: 5g*
- *Cholesterol: 180mg*
- *Sodium: 290mg*
- *Potassium: 500mg*

Roasted Tomato and Garlic Pasta

Yield: *4 servings*
Preparation Time: *10 minutes*
Cooking Time: *30 minutes*

Ingredients:

- 1 pound cherry tomatoes
- 1 head garlic
- 3 tablespoons olive oil
- 12 ounces whole wheat pasta (spaghetti or penne)
- Salt and pepper to taste
- 1/4 teaspoon red pepper flakes (optional)
- 1/4 cup fresh basil, chopped (for garnish)
- Grated Parmesan cheese (optional, for serving)

Instructions:

1. Preheat the oven to 400°F (200°C) and place cherry tomatoes on a baking sheet; cut the top off the garlic head, drizzle with 1 tablespoon olive oil, wrap in foil, and add it to the sheet.
2. Roast the tomatoes and garlic for 25-30 minutes until the tomatoes burst and the garlic is soft.
3. Meanwhile, cook the pasta according to package instructions; drain and reserve 1/2 cup of the pasta water.
4. Squeeze the roasted garlic into a large bowl, mash it, and mix in the roasted tomatoes, remaining olive oil, red pepper flakes, salt, and pepper; add the pasta and toss to combine, using reserved pasta water to loosen the sauce if necessary.
5. Serve hot, garnished with fresh basil and grated Parmesan, if desired.

Nutritional Information (per serving):

- **Calories:** *320*
- **Protein:** *12g*
- **Carbohydrates:** *45g*
- **Fats:** *12g*
- **Fiber:** *4g*
- **Cholesterol:** *5mg*
- **Sodium:** *250mg*
- **Potassium:** *450mg*

Saffron Rice with Peas and Carrots

Yield: *4 servings*
Preparation Time: *10 minutes*
Cooking Time: *20 minutes*

Ingredients:

- 1 cup long-grain rice (such as basmati)
- 2 cups vegetable broth or water
- 1/2 teaspoon saffron threads
- 1 cup frozen peas
- 1 cup carrots, diced
- 2 tablespoons olive oil
- Salt and pepper to taste
- Fresh parsley, chopped (for garnish)

Instructions:

1. In a small bowl, soak saffron threads in 2 tablespoons of hot water for about 10 minutes.
2. In a medium pot, heat olive oil over medium heat, add the diced carrots, and cook for 3-4 minutes until softened.
3. Add the rice to the pot and toast for 1-2 minutes, then stir in the vegetable broth, saffron water (with threads), peas, salt, and pepper.
4. Bring to a boil, reduce heat to low, cover, and simmer for 15-18 minutes until the rice is tender and the liquid is absorbed.
5. Fluff the rice with a fork, garnish with fresh parsley, and serve warm.

Nutritional Information (per serving):

- **Calories:** *220*
- **Protein:** *5g*
- **Carbohydrates:** *36g*
- **Fats:** *7g*
- **Fiber:** *3g*
- **Cholesterol:** *0mg*
- **Sodium:** *200mg*
- **Potassium:** *350mg*

Farro with Mushrooms and Thyme

Yield: *4 servings*
Preparation Time: *10 minutes*
Cooking Time: *30 minutes*

Ingredients:

- 1 cup farro
- 3 cups vegetable broth or water
- 2 tablespoons olive oil
- 8 ounces mushrooms, sliced (such as cremini or button)
- 2 cloves garlic, minced
- 1 teaspoon fresh thyme (or 1/2 teaspoon dried thyme)
- Salt and pepper to taste
- Fresh parsley, chopped (for garnish)

Instructions:

1. Rinse the farro under cold water and then combine it with the vegetable broth in a pot; bring to a boil, reduce heat, cover, and simmer for 20-25 minutes until tender, then drain if necessary.
2. In a large skillet, heat olive oil over medium heat and add the sliced mushrooms; sauté for 5-7 minutes until they are browned and tender.
3. Add minced garlic and thyme to the skillet, cooking for an additional minute until fragrant.
4. Stir the cooked farro into the skillet, seasoning with salt and pepper to taste, and mix until heated through.
5. Serve warm, garnished with fresh parsley.

Nutritional Information (per serving):

- *Calories: 240*
- *Protein: 8g*
- *Carbohydrates: 43g*
- *Fats: 6g*
- *Fiber: 7g*
- *Cholesterol: 0mg*
- *Sodium: 150mg*
- *Potassium: 370mg*

Roasted Vegetable and Pesto Pasta

Yield: *4 servings*
Preparation Time: *15 minutes*
Cooking Time: *30 minutes*

Ingredients:

- 8 ounces whole wheat pasta (like penne or fusilli)
- 2 cups mixed vegetables (bell peppers, zucchini, cherry tomatoes, and eggplant)
- 2 tablespoons olive oil
- Salt and pepper to taste
- 1/2 cup homemade or store-bought basil pesto
- Grated Parmesan cheese (optional, for serving)
- Fresh basil leaves (for garnish)

Instructions:

1. Preheat the oven to 425°F (220°C). Toss the mixed vegetables with olive oil, salt and pepper on a baking sheet, then roast for 20-25 minutes until tender and slightly charred.
2. Meanwhile, cook the pasta according to package instructions until al dente; drain and reserve 1/2 cup of pasta water.
3. In a large bowl, combine the cooked pasta, roasted vegetables, and pesto; mix well, adding reserved pasta water a little at a time to reach desired consistency.
4. Serve warm, topped with grated Parmesan cheese if desired, and garnish with fresh basil leaves.
5. Enjoy as a nutritious main dish or side, highlighting the vibrant flavors of the Mediterranean.

Nutritional Information (per serving):
- *Calories: 320*
- *Protein: 10g*
- *Carbohydrates: 45g*
- *Fats: 12g*
- *Fiber: 6g*
- *Cholesterol: 5mg (if using Parmesan)*
- *Sodium: 180mg*
- *Potassium: 550mg*

Feta and Spinach Stuffed Ravioli

Yield: 4 servings
Preparation Time: 30 minutes
Cooking Time: 15 minutes

Ingredients:

- **For the filling:**
  - 1 cup fresh spinach, chopped
  - 1/2 cup feta cheese, crumbled
  - 1/4 cup ricotta cheese
  - 1 clove garlic, minced
  - 1 tablespoon olive oil
  - Salt and pepper to taste
  - 1/4 teaspoon nutmeg (optional)
- **For the ravioli:**
  - 12-16 wonton wrappers or homemade pasta sheets
  - 1 tablespoon water (for sealing)

Instructions:

1. In a skillet, heat olive oil over medium heat and sauté garlic until fragrant; add chopped spinach and cook until wilted, about 2-3 minutes.
2. In a bowl, mix the cooked spinach with feta, ricotta, salt, pepper, and nutmeg until well combined.
3. Place about 1 tablespoon of the filling in the center of each wonton wrapper, moisten the edges with water, fold over, and seal tightly to form ravioli.
4. Bring a large pot of salted water to a boil, then cook the ravioli for 3-4 minutes until they float; drain and set aside.
5. Serve topped with warm marinara sauce, garnished with fresh basil and Parmesan, if desired, for a delightful Mediterranean meal.

Nutritional Information (per serving):

- **Calories:** *320*
- **Protein:** *12g*
- **Carbohydrates:** *35g*
- **Fats:** *14g*
- **Fiber:** *3g*
- **Cholesterol:** *35mg*
- **Sodium:** *500mg*
- **Potassium:** *400mg*

Bulgur with Herbs and Pine Nuts

Yield: 4 servings
Preparation Time: 10 minutes
Cooking Time: 15 minutes

Ingredients:

- 1 cup bulgur wheat
- 2 cups vegetable broth or water
- 1/4 cup pine nuts
- 1/4 cup fresh parsley, finely chopped
- 1/4 cup fresh mint, finely chopped
- 1 clove garlic, minced
- 2 tablespoons olive oil
- Juice of 1 lemon
- Salt and pepper to taste

Instructions:

1. In a saucepan, bring the vegetable broth (or water) to a boil, add the bulgur, cover, and simmer for 12-15 minutes until tender and water is absorbed; fluff with a fork.
2. Meanwhile, toast the pine nuts in a dry skillet over medium heat for 3-4 minutes until golden, stirring frequently.
3. In a large bowl, combine cooked bulgur, toasted pine nuts, parsley, mint, garlic, olive oil, lemon juice, salt, and pepper, mixing well to combine.
4. Adjust seasoning to taste and let the mixture sit for 5 minutes to allow the flavors to meld.
5. Serve warm or at room temperature as a flavorful side dish or light main course.

Nutritional Information (per serving):

- **Calories:** *220*
- **Protein:** *6g*
- **Carbohydrates:** *35g*
- **Fats:** *8g*
- **Fiber:** *5g*
- **Cholesterol:** *0mg*
- **Sodium:** *200mg*
- **Potassium:** *300mg*

Eggplant and Olive Baked Pasta

Yield: 6 servings
Preparation Time: 15 minutes
Cooking Time: 30 minutes

Ingredients:
- 12 ounces whole wheat penne pasta
- 1 large eggplant, diced
- 1 cup black olives, pitted and sliced
- 1 can (14 ounces) diced tomatoes, drained
- 1/2 cup ricotta cheese
- 1/2 cup grated Parmesan cheese
- 2 cloves garlic, minced
- 2 tablespoons olive oil
- 1 teaspoon dried oregano
- 1 teaspoon dried basil
- Salt and pepper to taste
- Fresh basil leaves for garnish (optional)

Instructions:
1. Preheat the oven to 375°F (190°C) and cook the pasta according to package instructions until al dente; drain and set aside.
2. In a large skillet, heat olive oil over medium heat, add diced eggplant, garlic, oregano, basil, salt, and pepper, and sauté for 5-7 minutes until eggplant is tender.
3. In a large bowl, combine cooked pasta, sautéed eggplant mixture, diced tomatoes, olives, ricotta cheese, and half of the Parmesan cheese; mix well.
4. Transfer the mixture to a greased 9x13-inch baking dish, sprinkle with the remaining Parmesan, and bake for 20 minutes until golden and bubbly.
5. Serve warm, garnished with fresh basil if desired, for a wholesome Mediterranean-inspired meal.

Nutritional Information (per serving):
- *Calories: 320*
- *Protein: 12g*
- *Carbohydrates: 40g*
- *Fats: 12g*
- *Fiber: 6g*
- *Cholesterol: 30mg*
- *Sodium: 350mg*
- *Potassium: 500mg*

Tomato and Basil Risotto

Yield: 4 servings
Preparation Time: 10 minutes
Cooking Time: 25 minutes

Ingredients:
- 1 cup Arborio rice
- 4 cups low-sodium vegetable broth
- 1 can (14 ounces) diced tomatoes, drained
- 1 small onion, finely chopped
- 2 cloves garlic, minced
- 1/2 cup grated Parmesan cheese
- 1/4 cup fresh basil leaves, chopped (plus extra for garnish)
- 2 tablespoons olive oil
- Salt and pepper to taste

Instructions:
1. In a saucepan, heat the vegetable broth over low heat and keep it warm. In a large skillet, heat olive oil over medium heat, then add the onion and garlic, sautéing until softened (about 3-4 minutes).
2. Stir in the Arborio rice and cook for 1-minutes until slightly toasted.
3. Gradually add the warm broth, one ladle a time, stirring continuously until the liquid is absorbed before adding more; this should take about 18-20 minutes.
4. Once the rice is creamy and al dente, stir in the drained diced tomatoes, Parmesan cheese, basil, salt, and pepper, cooking for an additional 2 minutes.
5. Serve warm, garnished with extra basil, for a fresh and hearty Mediterranean-inspired dish.

Nutritional Information (per serving):
- *Calories: 320*
- *Protein: 10g*
- *Carbohydrates: 46g*
- *Fats: 10g*
- *Fiber: 3g*
- *Cholesterol: 5mg*
- *Sodium: 250mg*
- *Potassium: 500mg*

Chickpea and Couscous Pilaf

Yield: 4 servings
Preparation Time: 10 minutes
Cooking Time: 15 minutes

Ingredients:

- 1 cup couscous
- 1 can (15 ounces) chickpeas, drained and rinsed
- 2 cups vegetable broth or water
- 1 small onion, finely chopped
- 2 cloves garlic, minced
- 1 teaspoon ground cumin
- 1 teaspoon smoked paprika
- 1/4 cup fresh parsley, chopped (or cilantro, optional)
- 2 tablespoons olive oil
- Salt and pepper to taste
- Lemon wedges for serving

Instructions:

1. In a medium saucepan, heat olive oil over medium heat, then add the onion and garlic, sautéing until softened (about 3-4 minutes).
2. Stir in the cumin and smoked paprika, cooking for an additional minute to release the flavors.
3. Add the vegetable broth and chickpeas, bringing the mixture to a boil; then stir in the couscous, remove from heat, and cover for 5 minutes.
4. Fluff the couscous with a fork and stir in the chopped parsley, salt, and pepper to taste.
5. Serve warm, garnished with lemon wedges for a bright flavor boost!

Nutritional Information (per serving):
- *Calories: 290*
- *Protein: 10g*
- *Carbohydrates: 45g*
- *Fats: 8g*
- *Fiber: 7g*
- *Cholesterol: 0mg*
- *Sodium: 300mg*
- *Potassium: 450mg*

Cumin-Spiced Basmati

Yield: 4 servings
Preparation Time: 10 minutes
Cooking Time: 20 minutes

Ingredients

- 1 cup basmati rice
- 2 cups vegetable broth (or water)
- 1 tablespoon olive oil
- 1 teaspoon ground cumin
- 1/2 teaspoon turmeric (optional, for color)
- 1/2 teaspoon salt (adjust to taste)
- 1/2 cup peas (fresh or frozen)
- 1/4 cup chopped fresh cilantro (optional)
- Lemon wedges for serving

Instructions

1. Rinse the basmati rice under cold water until the water runs clear, then drain well.
2. In a medium saucepan, heat the olive oil over medium heat, add the cumin and turmeric, and sauté for about 30 seconds until fragrant.
3. Add the rinsed rice and stir to coat with the oil and spices, then pour in the vegetable broth and salt; bring to a boil.
4. Reduce heat to low, cover, and simmer for about 15 minutes or until the rice is tender and the liquid is absorbed; stir in the peas during the last 5 minutes of cooking.
5. Fluff the rice with a fork, stir in cilantro if using, and serve with lemon wedges.

Nutritional Information (per serving)

- *Calories: 210*
- *Protein: 5g*
- *Carbohydrates: 36g*
- *Fats: 6g*
- *Fiber: 2g*
- *Cholesterol: 0mg*
- *Sodium: 320mg*
- *Potassium: 250mg*

Roasted Red Pepper Couscous Re

Yield: 4 servings
Preparation Time: 10 minutes
Cooking Time: 15 minutes

Ingredients

- 1 cup couscous
- 1 1/4 cups vegetable broth (or water)
- 1 large roasted red pepper, diced (store-bought or homemade)
- 2 tablespoons olive oil
- 1 clove garlic, minced
- 1/2 teaspoon smoked paprika (or regular paprika)
- 1/4 teaspoon salt (adjust to taste)
- 1/4 cup chopped fresh parsley (or basil for variation)
- Lemon wedges for serving

Instructions

1. In a medium saucepan, bring the vegetable broth to a boil, then remove from heat and stir in th couscous, cover, and let sit for 5 minutes until the liquid is absorbed.
2. Meanwhile, heat the olive oil in a skillet over medium heat, add the minced garlic, and sauté for minute until fragrant.
3. Stir in the diced roasted red pepper, smoked paprika, and salt, cooking for another 2-3 minutes unt heated through.
4. Fluff the couscous with a fork and combine it with the red pepper mixture, then fold in the choppe parsley.
5. Serve warm, garnished with lemon wedges.

Nutritional Information (per serving)

- *Calories:* 180
- *Protein:* 5g
- *Carbohydrates:* 30g
- *Fats:* 7g
- *Fiber:* 2g
- *Cholesterol:* 0mg
- *Sodium:* 290mg
- *Potassium:* 220mg

CHAPTER 6: FISH AND SEAFOOD

Grilled Lemon Herb Shrimp Skewers

Yield: *4 servings*
Preparation Time: *15 minutes*
Cooking Time: *10 minutes*

Ingredients

- 1 pound large shrimp, peeled and deveined
- 3 tablespoons olive oil
- Juice of 1 lemon (about 3 tablespoons)
- Zest of 1 lemon
- 3 cloves garlic, minced
- 1 tablespoon fresh parsley, chopped (or 1 teaspoon dried parsley)
- 1 tablespoon fresh oregano, chopped (or 1 teaspoon dried oregano)
- Salt and pepper to taste
- Wooden or metal skewers (if using wooden skewers, soak in water for 30 minutes before use)

Instructions

1. In a bowl, whisk together olive oil, lemon juice, lemon zest, garlic, parsley, oregano, salt, and pepper to create a marinade.
2. Add the shrimp to the marinade, tossing to coat, and let it marinate for at least 15 minutes.
3. Preheat a grill or grill pan over medium-high heat and thread the shrimp onto the skewers.
4. Grill the skewers for 2-3 minutes on each side, until the shrimp are pink and opaque.
5. Serve warm with lemon wedges and a side of salad or whole grain for a complete meal.

Nutritional Information (per serving)

- **Calories:** *210*
- **Protein:** *25g*
- **Carbohydrates:** *1g*
- **Fats:** *12g*
- **Fiber:** *0g*
- **Cholesterol:** *165mg*
- **Sodium:** *270mg*
- **Potassium:** *320mg*

Baked Cod with Olive and Tomato Relish

Yield: *4 servings*
Preparation Time: *15 minutes*
Cooking Time: *20 minutes*

Ingredients

- 4 (6-ounce) cod fillets
- 2 tablespoons olive oil
- 1 cup cherry tomatoes, halved
- 1/2 cup pitted black olives, chopped
- 2 cloves garlic, minced
- 1 tablespoon capers, rinsed and drained
- 1 teaspoon dried oregano
- Salt and pepper to taste
- Fresh basil or parsley for garnish

Instructions

1. Preheat the oven to 400°F (200°C) and lightly grease a baking dish with olive oil.
2. Place the cod fillets in the baking dish, seasoning with salt, pepper, and oregano.
3. In a bowl, mix together the cherry tomatoes, olives, garlic, capers, and a drizzle of olive oil, then spoon the mixture over the cod.
4. Bake for 20 minutes, or until the cod is opaque and flakes easily with a fork.
5. Serve the baked cod garnished with fresh basil or parsley, alongside a side of whole grains or a green salad.

Nutritional Information (per serving)

- **Calories:** *280*
- **Protein:** *30g*
- **Carbohydrates:** *8g*
- **Fats:** *14g*
- **Fiber:** *2g*
- **Cholesterol:** *75mg*
- **Sodium:** *350mg*
- **Potassium:** *650mg*

Mediterranean Tuna Salad with Capers

Yield: *4 servings*
Preparation Time: *15 minutes*
Cooking Time: *0 minutes (no cooking required)*

Ingredients

- 2 (5-ounce) cans of tuna in water, drained
- 1/2 cup cherry tomatoes, halved
- 1/3 cup red onion, finely chopped
- 1/4 cup Kalamata olives, pitted and sliced
- 2 tablespoons capers, rinsed
- 1/4 cup fresh parsley, chopped
- 3 tablespoons olive oil
- 1 tablespoon red wine vinegar
- 1 teaspoon dried oregano
- Salt and pepper to taste

Instructions

1. In a large bowl, combine the drained tuna, cherry tomatoes, red onion, olives, capers, and parsley.
2. In a small bowl, whisk together the olive oil, red wine vinegar, oregano, salt, and pepper.
3. Pour the dressing over the tuna mixture and gently toss until well combined.
4. Adjust seasoning if necessary and let the salad sit for 5 minutes to allow the flavors to meld.
5. Serve chilled or at room temperature, with whole-grain crackers or on a bed of greens.

Nutritional Information (per serving)

- *Calories: 220*
- *Protein: 25g*
- *Carbohydrates: 8g*
- *Fats: 10g*
- *Fiber: 2g*
- *Cholesterol: 45mg*
- *Sodium: 400mg*
- *Potassium: 500mg*

Grilled Octopus with Lemon and Parsley

Yield: *4 servings*
Preparation Time: *20 minutes*
Cooking Time: *15 minutes*

Ingredients

- 1 1/2 pounds octopus, cleaned
- 1/4 cup olive oil
- 3 cloves garlic, minced
- 1 lemon, zested and juiced
- 1/4 cup fresh parsley, chopped
- Salt and black pepper to taste
- 1 teaspoon red pepper flakes (optional)

Instructions

1. In a large pot, bring salted water to a boil and add the octopus; simmer for about 4 minutes until tender, then drain and let cool.
2. Once cooled, cut the tentacles into manageable pieces and place them in bowl with olive oil, garlic, lemon zest, lemon juice, salt, pepper, and red pepper flakes.
3. Preheat a grill or grill pan over medium high heat, then grill the octopus pieces for about 3-4 minutes per side until charred and slightly crispy.
4. Remove from the grill and let rest for couple of minutes, then toss with fresh parsley before serving.
5. Serve hot, drizzled with extra olive oil and lemon wedges on the side.

Nutritional Information (per serving)

- *Calories: 260*
- *Protein: 30g*
- *Carbohydrates: 4g*
- *Fats: 14g*
- *Fiber: 0g*
- *Cholesterol: 80mg*
- *Sodium: 300mg*
- *Potassium: 600mg*

Saffron Mussels with Garlic and White Wine

Yield: *4 servings*
Preparation Time: *10 minutes*
Cooking Time: *15 minutes*

Ingredients

- 2 pounds fresh mussels, cleaned and debearded
- 2 tablespoons olive oil
- 4 cloves garlic, minced
- 1 cup dry white wine (such as Sauvignon Blanc)
- 1/4 teaspoon saffron threads
- 1/4 cup fresh parsley, chopped
- Salt and black pepper to taste
- Lemon wedges for serving

Instructions

1. In a large pot, heat olive oil over medium heat and sauté the minced garlic until fragrant, about 1 minute.
2. Add the white wine and saffron threads to the pot, bringing the mixture to a simmer.
3. Stir in the cleaned mussels, cover the pot, and steam for about 5-7 minutes, or until the mussels have opened.
4. Remove from heat, season with salt, pepper, and stir in the chopped parsley.
5. Serve immediately with lemon wedges and crusty bread for dipping.

Nutritional Information (per serving)

- *Calories: 240*
- *Protein: 25g*
- *Carbohydrates: 6g*
- *Fats: 12g*
- *Fiber: 0g*
- *Cholesterol: 50mg*
- *Sodium: 300mg*
- *Potassium: 450mg*

Shrimp and Artichoke Pasta

Yield: *4 servings*
Preparation Time: *10 minutes*
Cooking Time: *15 minutes*

Ingredients

- 8 ounces whole wheat pasta (spaghetti or penne)
- 1 pound shrimp, peeled and deveined
- 1 can (14 ounces) artichoke hearts, drained and quartered
- 3 tablespoons olive oil
- 3 cloves garlic, minced
- 1/2 teaspoon red pepper flakes (optional)
- 1/2 cup cherry tomatoes, halved
- 1/4 cup fresh parsley, chopped
- Juice of 1 lemon
- Salt and black pepper to taste

Instructions

1. Cook the pasta according to package instructions; drain and set aside.
2. In a large skillet, heat olive oil over medium heat and sauté minced garlic and red pepper flakes until fragrant, about 1 minute.
3. Add shrimp and cook for 3-4 minutes until pink, then stir in artichokes and cherry tomatoes, cooking for an additional 2 minutes.
4. Combine the cooked pasta with the shrimp mixture, tossing in lemon juice, chopped parsley, salt, and pepper to taste.
5. Serve warm, garnished with extra parsley, if desired.

Nutritional Information (per serving)

- *Calories: 360*
- *Protein: 28g*
- *Carbohydrates: 48g*
- *Fats: 10g*
- *Fiber: 6g*
- *Cholesterol: 150mg*
- *Sodium: 360mg*
- *Potassium: 620mg*

Baked Salmon with Spinach and Feta

Yield: 4 servings
Preparation Time: 10 minutes
Cooking Time: 20 minutes

Ingredients

- 4 salmon fillets (6 ounces each)
- 4 cups fresh spinach, chopped
- 1/2 cup feta cheese, crumbled
- 2 tablespoons olive oil
- 2 cloves garlic, minced
- 1 teaspoon dried oregano
- Juice of 1 lemon
- Salt and pepper to taste
- Optional: cherry tomatoes for garnish

Instructions

1. Preheat your oven to 375°F (190°C) and grease a baking dish with olive oil.
2. In a skillet over medium heat, sauté minced garlic in 1 tablespoon of olive oil until fragrant, then add the chopped spinach and cook until wilted; season with salt, pepper, and oregano.
3. Place the salmon fillets in the baking dish and top each with the sautéed spinach and crumbled feta, then drizzle with lemon juice and remaining olive oil.
4. Bake for 15-20 minutes, or until the salmon is cooked through and flakes easily with a fork.
5. Serve warm, garnished with cherry tomatoes if desired.

Nutritional Information (per serving)

- *Calories: 320*
- *Protein: 34g*
- *Carbohydrates: 4g*
- *Fats: 18g*
- *Fiber: 2g*
- *Cholesterol: 80mg*
- *Sodium: 450mg*
- *Potassium: 600mg*

Seared Scallops with Herb Butter

Yield: 4 servings
Preparation Time: 10 minutes
Cooking Time: 10 minutes

Ingredients

- 1 pound large sea scallops (about 16-20 scallops)
- 2 tablespoons olive oil
- 4 tablespoons unsalted butter
- 2 cloves garlic, minced
- 2 tablespoons fresh parsley, chopped
- 1 tablespoon fresh basil, chopped
- Juice of 1 lemon
- Salt and pepper to taste

Instructions

1. Pat the scallops dry with paper towels and season with salt and pepper.
2. In a large skillet, heat olive oil over medium-high heat until shimmering; add scallops and sear for 2-3 minutes on each side until golden brown and opaque.
3. Remove the scallops from the skillet and set aside.
4. In the same skillet, melt the butter and add minced garlic, cooking until fragrant, then stir in parsley, basil, lemon juice, and season to taste.
5. Return the scallops to the skillet, gently tossing them in the herb butter before serving warm.

Nutritional Information (per serving)

- *Calories: 250*
- *Protein: 27g*
- *Carbohydrates: 2g*
- *Fats: 15g*
- *Fiber: 0g*
- *Cholesterol: 60mg*
- *Sodium: 300mg*
- *Potassium: 450mg*

Red Snapper with Olives and Capers

Yield: 4 servings
Preparation Time: 10 minutes
Cooking Time: 20 minutes

Ingredients

- 4 red snapper fillets (about 6 ounces each)
- 2 tablespoons olive oil
- 1 cup cherry tomatoes, halved
- 1/2 cup green olives, pitted and sliced
- 2 tablespoons capers, rinsed
- 2 cloves garlic, minced
- Juice of 1 lemon
- 1 teaspoon dried oregano
- Salt and pepper to taste

Instructions

1. Preheat the oven to 375°F (190°C) and lightly grease a baking dish with olive oil.
2. Arrange the red snapper fillets in the baking dish, seasoning with salt, pepper, and oregano.
3. In a bowl, combine the cherry tomatoes, olives, capers, garlic, lemon juice, and a drizzle of olive oil; mix well and spoon the mixture over the fillets.
4. Bake in the preheated oven for 15-20 minutes, or until the fish flakes easily with a fork.
5. Garnish with fresh parsley and serve hot, ideally with a side of steamed vegetables or a light salad.

Nutritional Information (per serving)
- **Calories:** *290*
- **Protein:** *28g*
- **Carbohydrates:** *6g*
- **Fats:** *18g*
- **Fiber:** *2g*
- **Cholesterol:** *80mg*
- **Sodium:** *600mg*
- **Potassium:** *600mg*

Grilled Sardines with Lemon and Rosemary

Yield: 4 servings
Preparation Time: 10 minutes
Cooking Time: 10 minutes

Ingredients

- 8 fresh sardines, cleaned and scaled
- 4 tablespoons olive oil
- 2 lemons (1 for juice and 1 sliced)
- 2 tablespoons fresh rosemary, chopped (or 1 tablespoon dried rosemary)
- Salt and pepper to taste

Instructions

1. Preheat the grill to medium-high heat and brush the grates with olive oil to prevent sticking.
2. Rinse the sardines under cold water and pat them dry; season inside and out with salt, pepper, and chopped rosemary.
3. Drizzle olive oil and the juice of one lemon over the sardines, ensuring they are well coated.
4. Grill the sardines for about 3-4 minutes on each side, adding lemon slices to the grill for added flavor.
5. Serve hot, drizzled with extra olive oil and accompanied by fresh lemon wedges and a green salad or grilled vegetables.

Nutritional Information (per serving)

- **Calories:** *280*
- **Protein:** *24g*
- **Carbohydrates:** *2g*
- **Fats:** *20g*
- **Fiber:** *0g*
- **Cholesterol:** *70mg*
- **Sodium:** *180mg*
- **Potassium:** *380mg*

Mediterranean Fish Stew with Saffron

Yield: *4 servings*
Preparation Time: *15 minutes*
Cooking Time: *30 minutes*

Ingredients
- 1 pound white fish fillets (such as cod or halibut), cut into chunks
- 1 tablespoon olive oil
- 1 onion, finely chopped
- 2 garlic cloves, minced
- 1 bell pepper, diced
- 1 can (14 oz) diced tomatoes
- 1 cup fish stock (or vegetable broth)
- 1 teaspoon saffron threads
- 1 teaspoon dried oregano
- Salt and pepper to taste

Instructions
1. In a large pot, heat olive oil over medium heat; sauté onions, garlic, and bell pepper until softened, about 5 minutes.
2. Add the diced tomatoes, fish stock, saffron, oregano, salt, and pepper; bring to a simmer for 10 minutes to develop flavors.
3. Gently add the fish chunks, cover, and cook for an additional 10-15 minutes until the fish is cooked through and flakes easily.
4. Taste and adjust seasoning as necessary, then remove from heat and let rest for a few minutes.
5. Serve hot, garnished with fresh parsley and lemon wedges, alongside crusty whole-grain bread.

Nutritional Information (per serving)
- **Calories:** *290*
- **Protein:** *28g*
- **Carbohydrates:** *16g*
- **Fats:** *12g*
- **Fiber:** *3g*
- **Cholesterol:** *50mg*
- **Sodium:** *400mg*
- **Potassium:** *700mg*

Garlic and Lemon Baked Tilapia

Yield: *4 servings*
Preparation Time: *10 minutes*
Cooking Time: *20 minutes*

Ingredients

- 4 tilapia fillets (about 6 ounces each)
- 3 tablespoons olive oil
- 3 garlic cloves, minced
- 1 lemon, juice and zest
- 1 teaspoon dried oregano
- Salt and pepper to taste
- Fresh parsley, chopped (for garnish)
- Lemon wedges (for serving)

Instructions

1. Preheat the oven to 400°F (200°C) and lightly grease a baking dish with olive oil.
2. In a bowl, whisk together the olive oil, minced garlic, lemon juice, lemon zest, oregano, salt, and pepper.
3. Place the tilapia fillets in the baking dish and pour the garlic-lemon mixture over the fish, ensuring they're well-coated.
4. Bake for 15-20 minutes or until the fish is opaque and flakes easily with a fork.
5. Serve garnished with fresh parsley and lemon wedges, alongside a side of steamed vegetables or whole grains.

Nutritional Information (per serving)

- **Calories:** *230*
- **Protein:** *28g*
- **Carbohydrates:** *4g*
- **Fats:** *12g*
- **Fiber:** *1g*
- **Cholesterol:** *70mg*
- **Sodium:** *180mg*
- **Potassium:** *520mg*

Shrimp Saganaki with Tomatoes and Feta

Yield: 4 servings
Preparation Time: 10 minutes
Cooking Time: 20 minutes

Ingredients

- 1 pound (450g) shrimp, peeled and deveined
- 2 tablespoons olive oil
- 1 medium onion, finely chopped
- 2 garlic cloves, minced
- 1 can (14 oz) diced tomatoes (or 2 cups fresh tomatoes, chopped)
- 1 teaspoon dried oregano
- 1/2 teaspoon red pepper flakes (optional)
- 4 ounces (113g) feta cheese, crumbled
- Fresh parsley, chopped (for garnish)
- Salt and pepper to taste

Instructions

1. In a large skillet, heat the olive oil over medium heat, then add the chopped onion and cook until softened, about 5 minutes.
2. Stir in the garlic and cook for another minute before adding the diced tomatoes, oregano, red pepper flakes, salt, and pepper; simmer for 5 minutes.
3. Add the shrimp to the skillet and cook until they turn pink, about 3-4 minutes, stirring occasionally.
4. Remove from heat and sprinkle crumbled feta on top; cover for a couple of minutes to let the cheese soften.
5. Serve warm, garnished with fresh parsley and lemon wedges, alongside crusty bread or a salad.

Nutritional Information (per serving)
- *Calories:* 280
- *Protein:* 24g
- *Carbohydrates:* 8g
- *Fats:* 18g
- *Fiber:* 2g
- *Cholesterol:* 150mg
- *Sodium:* 570mg
- *Potassium:* 450mg

Baked Sole with Fresh Herbs

Yield: 4 servings
Preparation Time: 10 minutes
Cooking Time: 20 minutes

Ingredients

- 4 sole fillets (about 6 oz each)
- 2 tablespoons olive oil
- 2 cloves garlic, minced
- 1 tablespoon fresh parsley, chopped
- 1 tablespoon fresh dill, chopped (or substitute with thyme or basil)
- Zest and juice of 1 lemon
- Salt and pepper to taste
- Lemon wedges for serving

Instructions

1. Preheat your oven to 375°F (190°C) and lightly grease a baking dish with olive oil.
2. In a small bowl, mix the olive oil, garlic, parsley, dill, lemon zest, and juice, then season with salt and pepper.
3. Place the sole fillets in the baking dish, then drizzle the herb mixture over the top, ensuring they are evenly coated.
4. Bake for 15-20 minutes, or until the fish is opaque and flakes easily with a fork.
5. Serve hot with lemon wedges and your choice of side salad or steamed vegetables.

Nutritional Information (per serving)
- *Calories:* 250
- *Protein:* 25g
- *Carbohydrates:* 3g
- *Fats:* 15g
- *Fiber:* 0g
- *Cholesterol:* 70mg
- *Sodium:* 220mg
- *Potassium:* 400mg

Spicy Calamari with Lemon Aioli

Yield: 4 servings
Preparation Time: 15 minutes
Cooking Time: 10 minutes

Ingredients

- **For the Calamari:**
  - 1 pound (450g) fresh calamari, cleaned and sliced into rings
  - 1/2 cup whole wheat flour (or gluten-free flour)
  - 1 teaspoon paprika
  - 1/2 teaspoon cayenne pepper (adjust to taste)
  - Salt and pepper to taste
  - 2 tablespoons olive oil
  - Lemon wedges (for serving)
- **For the Lemon Aioli:**
  - 1/2 cup Greek yogurt
  - 2 tablespoons mayonnaise (optional)
  - 2 cloves garlic, minced
  - 1 tablespoon lemon juice
  - 1 teaspoon lemon zest
  - Salt and pepper to taste
  - Fresh parsley, chopped (for garnish)

Instructions

1. In a bowl, combine flour, paprika, cayenne, salt, and pepper; dredge the calamari rings in the mixture.
2. Heat olive oil in a skillet over medium-high heat and fry the calamari for about 2-3 minutes until golden and crispy; drain on paper towels.
3. For the aioli, mix Greek yogurt, mayonnaise, minced garlic, lemon juice, lemon zest, salt, and pepper in a small bowl until well combined.
4. Serve the spicy calamari hot with a side of lemon aioli and lemon wedges.
5. Garnish with chopped parsley before serving.

Nutritional Information (per serving)

- **Calories:** 280
- **Protein:** 23g
- **Carbohydrates:** 18g
- **Fats:** 14g
- **Fiber:** 1g
- **Cholesterol:** 140mg
- **Sodium:** 400mg
- **Potassium:** 450mg

Roasted Sea Bass with Olive Tapenade

Yield: 4 servings
Preparation Time: 15 minutes
Cooking Time: 20 minutes

Ingredients

- **For the Sea Bass:**
  - 4 (6-ounce) sea bass fillets, skin on
  - 2 tablespoons olive oil
  - Salt and pepper to taste
  - 1 lemon, sliced
- **For the Olive Tapenade:**
  - 1 cup mixed olives (e.g., Kalamata and green), pitted
  - 2 tablespoons capers, rinsed
  - 2 cloves garlic, minced
  - 2 tablespoons fresh parsley, chopped
  - 1 tablespoon lemon juice
  - 1 tablespoon olive oil
  - Fresh herbs (like thyme or oregano) for customization

Instructions

1. Preheat the oven to 400°F (200°C) and line a baking sheet with parchment paper.
2. Place the sea bass fillets on the prepared baking sheet, drizzle with olive oil, season with salt and pepper, and top with lemon slices; roast for 15-20 minutes until cooked through.
3. Meanwhile, prepare the olive tapenade by combining olives, capers, garlic, parsley, lemon juice, and olive oil in a food

processor; blend until chunky and well combined.

4. Once the fish is done, remove from the oven and let it rest for a couple of minutes.

5. Serve the roasted sea bass topped with the olive tapenade and garnish with additional parsley if desired.

Nutritional Information (per serving)

- **Calories:** 350
- **Protein:** 30g
- **Carbohydrates:** 6g
- **Fats:** 23g
- **Fiber:** 2g
- **Cholesterol:** 85mg
- **Sodium:** 600mg
- **Potassium:** 550mg

Lobster and Tomato Risotto

Yield: 4 servings
Preparation Time: 15 minutes
Cooking Time: 30 minutes

Ingredients

- 1 cup Arborio rice
- 1 medium onion, finely chopped
- 2 cloves garlic, minced
- 4 cups low-sodium chicken or vegetable broth
- 1 cup dry white wine
- 2 tablespoons olive oil
- 1 cup cherry tomatoes, halved
- 1 cup cooked lobster meat, chopped
- 1/2 cup grated Parmesan cheese (optional)
- Salt and pepper to taste
- Fresh basil or parsley for garnish

Instructions

1. In a saucepan, heat the broth over low heat; in a large skillet, heat olive oil over medium heat and sauté the onion and garlic until softened, about 5 minutes.

2. Add Arborio rice to the skillet and cook, stirring frequently, for about 2 minutes until the rice is lightly toasted.

3. Pour in the white wine and stir until absorbed; gradually add the warm broth, one ladle at a time, stirring continuously until the rice is creamy and cooked al dente, about 18-20 minutes.

4. Stir in the cherry tomatoes and lobster meat, cooking for an additional 2-3 minutes until heated through; season with salt, pepper, and optional Parmesan cheese.

5. Serve the risotto hot, garnished with fresh basil or parsley.

Nutritional Information (per serving)

- **Calories:** 450
- **Protein:** 28g
- **Carbohydrates:** 56g
- **Fats:** 12g
- **Fiber:** 2g
- **Cholesterol:** 85mg
- **Sodium:** 600mg
- **Potassium:** 800mg

CHAPTER 7: POULTY RECIPES

Lemon and Herb Roasted Chicken

Yield: 4 servings
Preparation Time: 15 minutes
Cooking Time: 1 hour

Ingredients

- 4 bone-in, skin-on chicken thighs (about 6 oz each)
- 2 tablespoons olive oil
- Zest and juice of 1 lemon
- 4 cloves garlic, minced
- 1 tablespoon fresh rosemary, chopped (or 1 teaspoon dried)
- 1 tablespoon fresh thyme, chopped (or 1 teaspoon dried)
- Salt and pepper to taste
- Optional: 1 teaspoon smoked paprika for added flavor

Instructions

1. Preheat your oven to 425°F (220°C) and grease a baking dish with olive oil.
2. In a bowl, whisk together the olive oil, lemon juice, lemon zest, garlic, rosemary, thyme, smoked paprika (if using), salt, and pepper.
3. Rub the mixture all over the chicken thighs, ensuring they're evenly coated.
4. Place the chicken in the baking dish, skin side up, and roast for 45-60 minutes until the skin is crispy and the chicken reaches an internal temperature of 165°F (74°C).
5. Let rest for 5 minutes before serving with a side of roasted vegetables or a fresh salad.

Nutritional Information (per serving)

- *Calories:* 320
- *Protein:* 25g
- *Carbohydrates:* 2g
- *Fats:* 24g
- *Fiber:* 0g
- *Cholesterol:* 110mg
- *Sodium:* 280mg
- *Potassium:* 450mg

Greek Chicken Souvlaki with Tzatziki

Yield: 4 servings
Preparation Time: 20 minutes
Marinating Time: 1 hour
Cooking Time: 10-15 minutes

Ingredients

For the Chicken Souvlaki:

- 1 lb (450 g) boneless, skinless chicken breast, cut into 1-inch cubes
- 3 tablespoons olive oil
- Juice of 1 lemon
- 2 cloves garlic, minced
- 1 teaspoon dried oregano
- 1 teaspoon paprika
- Salt and pepper to taste
- Wooden or metal skewers (if using wooden, soak in water for 30 minutes)

For the Tzatziki Sauce:

- 1 cup plain Greek yogurt
- 1 small cucumber, grated and drained
- 2 cloves garlic, minced
- Juice of 1/2 lemon
- 1 tablespoon olive oil
- 1 tablespoon fresh dill, chopped (or 1 teaspoon dried)
- Salt to taste

Instructions

1. In a bowl, combine olive oil, lemon juice, garlic, oregano, paprika, salt, and pepper, then add chicken cubes and marinate for at least 1 hour in the refrigerator.
2. While the chicken is marinating, prepare the tzatziki sauce by mixing Greek yogurt, grated cucumber, garlic, lemon juice, olive oil, dill, and salt in a bowl; refrigerate until ready to serve.
3. Preheat your grill or grill pan over medium-high heat, and thread the marinated chicken onto skewers.
4. Grill the chicken skewers for 10-15 minutes, turning occasionally, until cooked through and slightly charred.
5. Serve the chicken souvlaki with tzatziki sauce, fresh pita, and a side salad or grilled vegetables.

Nutritional Information (per serving)

- **Calories:** 290
- **Protein:** 32g
- **Carbohydrates:** 7g
- **Fats:** 15g
- **Fiber:** 1g
- **Cholesterol:** 85mg
- **Sodium:** 320mg
- **Potassium:** 520mg

Chicken with Olives and Artichokes

Yield: *4 servings*
Preparation Time: *15 minutes*
Cooking Time: *30 minutes*

Ingredients

- 1 lb (450 g) boneless, skinless chicken thighs, cut into bite-sized pieces
- 2 tablespoons olive oil
- 3 cloves garlic, minced
- 1 cup cherry tomatoes, halved
- 1 can (14 oz) artichoke hearts, drained and quartered
- 1/2 cup Kalamata olives, pitted and halved
- 1 teaspoon dried oregano
- 1 teaspoon dried thyme
- Salt and pepper to taste
- Juice of 1 lemon
- Fresh parsley, chopped (for garnish)

Instructions

1. In a large skillet, heat olive oil over medium heat, then add the chicken and season with salt, pepper, oregano, and thyme; cook until browned and cooked through, about 7-10 minutes.
2. Add minced garlic and cook for another minute until fragrant.
3. Stir in cherry tomatoes, artichoke hearts, and olives, cooking for an additional 5-7 minutes until the tomatoes are softened.
4. Squeeze lemon juice over the mixture, stirring well to combine.
5. Garnish with fresh parsley and serve hot, ideally with whole grain bread or over a bed of quinoa.

Nutritional Information (per serving)
- **Calories:** *350*
- **Protein:** *30g*
- **Carbohydrates:** *14g*
- **Fats:** *18g*
- **Fiber:** *4g*
- **Cholesterol:** *80mg*
- **Sodium:** *600mg*
- **Potassium:** *550mg*

Pomegranate Glazed Chicken Thighs

Yield: *4 servings*
Preparation Time: *10 minutes*
Cooking Time: *30 minutes*

Ingredients

- 1 lb (450 g) bone-in, skin-on chicken thighs
- 1 cup pomegranate juice (preferably 100% pure)
- 2 tablespoons honey (or maple syrup for a vegan option)
- 1 tablespoon balsamic vinegar
- 2 cloves garlic, minced
- 1 teaspoon dried thyme (or 1 tablespoon fresh thyme)
- Salt and pepper to taste
- Pomegranate seeds (for garnish)

Instructions

1. Preheat the oven to 400°F (200°C) and season the chicken thighs with salt, pepper, and dried thyme.
2. In a small saucepan, combine pomegranate juice, honey, balsamic vinegar, and minced garlic; bring to a simmer and cook until slightly thickened, about 10 minutes.
3. Heat an oven-safe skillet over medium-high heat and sear the chicken thighs skin-side down for 5-7 minutes until golden brown.
4. Flip the chicken, pour the pomegranate glaze over the thighs, and transfer the skillet to the preheated oven; bake for 20 minutes or until the internal temperature reaches 165°F (74°C).
5. Garnish with pomegranate seeds and fresh parsley before serving, and enjoy with a side of quinoa or roasted vegetables.

Nutritional Information (per serving)
- **Calories:** *290*
- **Protein:** *24g*
- **Carbohydrates:** *18g*
- **Fats:** *15g*
- **Fiber:** *1g*
- **Cholesterol:** *95mg*
- **Sodium:** *350mg*
- **Potassium:** *350mg*

Chicken and Chickpea Stew with Spinach

Yield: 4 servings
Preparation Time: 10 minutes
Cooking Time: 30 minutes

Ingredients

- 1 lb (450 g) boneless, skinless chicken thighs, cut into bite-sized pieces
- 1 can (15 oz) chickpeas, rinsed and drained
- 4 cups fresh spinach, chopped
- 1 medium onion, finely chopped
- 3 cloves garlic, minced
- 1 can (14 oz) diced tomatoes, with juices
- 1 teaspoon ground cumin
- 1 teaspoon paprika
- 1 teaspoon dried oregano
- 2 tablespoons olive oil
- Salt and pepper to taste
- Lemon wedges (for serving)

Instructions

1. In a large pot, heat olive oil over medium heat and sauté the onion until translucent, about 5 minutes; add garlic and cook for an additional minute.
2. Stir in the chicken pieces, cumin, paprika, oregano, salt, and pepper; cook until the chicken is browned on all sides, about 5-7 minutes.
3. Add the diced tomatoes (with their juices) and chickpeas to the pot; bring to a simmer, cover, and cook for 15 minutes.
4. Stir in the chopped spinach and cook until wilted, about 2-3 minutes; adjust seasoning if needed.
5. Serve the stew with lemon wedges on the side for squeezing over the top, enhancing the flavors.

Nutritional Information (per serving)
- *Calories:* 320
- *Protein:* 28g
- *Carbohydrates:* 36g
- *Fats:* 8g
- *Fiber:* 10g
- *Cholesterol:* 75mg
- *Sodium:* 320mg
- *Potassium:* 750mg

Mediterranean Chicken and Orzo Bake

Yield: 4 servings
Preparation Time: 15 minutes
Cooking Time: 30 minutes

Ingredients

- 1 lb (450 g) boneless, skinless chicken breasts, cut into cubes
- 1 cup orzo pasta
- 2 cups low-sodium chicken broth
- 1 cup cherry tomatoes, halved
- 1 cup spinach, chopped
- 1/2 cup Kalamata olives, pitted and sliced
- 1/2 cup feta cheese, crumbled
- 2 tablespoons olive oil
- 1 teaspoon dried oregano
- 1 teaspoon garlic powder
- Salt and pepper to taste
- Fresh parsley (for garnish)

Instructions

1. Preheat the oven to 375°F (190°C) and lightly grease a baking dish.
2. In a large bowl, combine the chicken, orzo, chicken broth, cherry tomatoes, spinach, olives, olive oil, oregano, garlic powder, salt, and pepper; mix well.
3. Transfer the mixture to the prepared baking dish and spread evenly; cover with foil and bake for 25 minutes.
4. Remove the foil, sprinkle feta cheese on top, and bake for an additional 5 minutes or until the chicken is cooked through and the orzo is tender.
5. Garnish with fresh parsley before serving.

Nutritional Information (per serving)
- *Calories:* 410
- *Protein:* 32g
- *Carbohydrates:* 38g
- *Fats:* 18g
- *Fiber:* 4g
- *Cholesterol:* 75mg
- *Sodium:* 620mg
- *Potassium:* 600mg

Balsamic Chicken with Roasted Tomatoes

Yield: 4 servings
Preparation Time: 10 minutes
Cooking Time: 25 minutes

Ingredients

- 4 boneless, skinless chicken breasts (about 1.5 lbs)
- 2 cups cherry tomatoes, halved
- 1/4 cup balsamic vinegar
- 3 tablespoons olive oil
- 2 cloves garlic, minced
- 1 teaspoon dried basil
- 1 teaspoon dried oregano
- Salt and pepper to taste
- Fresh basil (for garnish)

Instructions

1. Preheat the oven to 400°F (200°C) and line a baking sheet with parchment paper.
2. In a small bowl, whisk together balsamic vinegar, olive oil, minced garlic, basil, oregano, salt, and pepper; set aside.
3. Place chicken breasts on the baking sheet, drizzle with half the balsamic mixture, and arrange cherry tomatoes around the chicken.
4. Roast in the oven for 20-25 minutes, or until the chicken is cooked through (165°F or 75°C) and tomatoes are blistered.
5. Drizzle the remaining balsamic mixture over the chicken and tomatoes, and garnish with fresh basil before serving.

Nutritional Information (per serving)

- *Calories: 320*
- *Protein: 35g*
- *Carbohydrates: 12g*
- *Fats: 15g*
- *Fiber: 2g*
- *Cholesterol: 80mg*
- *Sodium: 250mg*
- *Potassium: 600mg*

Herb-Crusted Chicken Breasts

Yield: 4 servings
Preparation Time: 15 minutes
Cooking Time: 25 minutes

Ingredients:

- **For the Chicken:**
  - 4 boneless, skinless chicken breasts (about 6 oz each)
  - 2 tbsp olive oil
  - 1 cup fresh breadcrumbs (preferably whole wheat)
  - ¼ cup grated Parmesan cheese
  - 1 tbsp fresh parsley, chopped (or 1 tsp dried)
  - 1 tbsp fresh thyme, chopped (or 1 tsp dried)
  - 1 tbsp fresh oregano, chopped (or 1 tsp dried)
  - 2 cloves garlic, minced
  - Salt and pepper to taste

Instructions:

1. Preheat the oven to 400°F (200°C) and lightly grease a baking sheet. In a bowl, combine breadcrumbs, Parmesan cheese, parsley, thyme, oregano, minced garlic, salt, and pepper.
2. Rub the chicken breasts with olive oil and season with salt and pepper, then coat each breast with the breadcrumb mixture, pressing gently to adhere.
3. Place the coated chicken breasts on the prepared baking sheet and bake for 20-25 minutes, or until the chicken is cooked through and the crust is golden brown.
4. Let the chicken rest for a few minutes before slicing to retain moisture.
5. Serve with a side of roasted vegetables or a fresh Mediterranean salad.

Nutritional Information (per serving):
- *Calories: 320*
- *Protein: 36g*
- *Carbohydrates: 10g*
- *Fats: 15g*
- *Fiber: 1g*
- *Cholesterol: 90mg*
- *Sodium: 450mg*
- *Potassium: 500mg*

Spicy Chicken Shawarma Wraps

Yield: *4 servings*
Preparation Time: *20 minutes*
Cooking Time: *20 minutes*

Ingredients:

- **For the Chicken Marinade:**
    - 1 lb (450g) boneless, skinless chicken thighs
    - 3 tbsp olive oil
    - 2 tbsp plain yogurt (Greek yogurt preferred)
    - 2 cloves garlic, minced
    - 1 tsp ground cumin
    - 1 tsp ground coriander
    - 1 tsp paprika
    - ½ tsp turmeric
    - ½ tsp cayenne pepper (adjust for spice level)
    - Salt and pepper to taste
- **For the Wraps:**
    - 4 whole wheat pita breads or wraps
    - 1 cup lettuce, shredded
    - 1 cup cucumber, diced
    - 1 cup tomatoes, diced
    - ½ cup red onion, thinly sliced
    - ½ cup tahini or garlic sauce (optional)
    - Fresh herbs (parsley or mint) for garnish

Instructions:

1. In a bowl, combine olive oil, yogurt, minced garlic, cumin, coriander, paprika, turmeric, cayenne, salt, and pepper to create a marinade. Add chicken thighs and marinate for at least 30 minutes (or overnight for deeper flavor).
2. Preheat a skillet over medium-high heat and cook the marinated chicken for about 6-7 minutes on each side until fully cooked and golden brown. Remove from heat and let it rest for a few minutes before slicing.
3. Warm the pita breads in a separate pan or oven for a few minutes until soft.
4. Assemble the wraps by placing sliced chicken on each pita, then top with lettuce, cucumber, tomatoes, red onion, and a drizzle of tahini or garlic sauce.
5. Roll up the wraps tightly and serve with fresh herbs for garnish.

Nutritional Information (per serving):

- *Calories: 450*
- *Protein: 30g*
- *Carbohydrates: 36g*
- *Fats: 20g*
- *Fiber: 6g*
- *Cholesterol: 75mg*
- *Sodium: 600mg*
- *Potassium: 750mg*

Lemon Garlic Chicken Skewers

Yield: *4 servings*
Preparation Time: *15 minutes*
Cooking Time: *15 minutes*

Ingredients:

- **For the Marinade:**
  - 1 lb (450g) boneless, skinless chicken breasts, cut into 1-inch cubes
  - ¼ cup olive oil
  - Juice and zest of 2 lemons
  - 4 cloves garlic, minced
  - 1 tsp dried oregano
  - 1 tsp dried thyme
  - Salt and pepper to taste
- **For the Skewers:**
  - 8 wooden or metal skewers (if using wooden, soak in water for 30 minutes to prevent burning)
  - 1 bell pepper, cut into 1-inch pieces (optional)
  - 1 red onion, cut into wedges (optional)
  - Fresh parsley for garnish

Instructions:

1. In a bowl, whisk together olive oil, lemon juice and zest, minced garlic, oregano, thyme, salt, and pepper to create the marinade. Add chicken cubes and marinate for at least 30 minutes (or up to 2 hours in the refrigerator for more flavor).
2. Preheat a grill or grill pan over medium-high heat. Thread the marinated chicken onto the skewers, alternating with bell pepper and onion pieces if using.
3. Grill the skewers for about 10-12 minutes, turning occasionally, until the chicken is cooked through and has nice grill marks.
4. Remove the skewers from the grill and let rest for a few minutes before serving.
5. Serve garnished with fresh parsley and a side of tzatziki sauce or a Mediterranean salad.

Nutritional Information (per serving):

- *Calories: 350*
- *Protein: 34g*
- *Carbohydrates: 6g*
- *Fats: 21g*
- *Fiber: 1g*
- *Cholesterol: 90mg*
- *Sodium: 400mg*
- *Potassium: 600mg*

Chicken Tagine with Preserved Lemons

Yield: 4 servings
Preparation Time: 15 minutes
Cooking Time: 1 hour

Ingredients:

- 1.5 lbs (680g) bone-in, skinless chicken thighs
- 2 tbsp olive oil
- 1 large onion, finely chopped
- 3 cloves garlic, minced
- 1 tsp ground cumin
- 1 tsp ground coriander
- 1 tsp ground cinnamon
- ½ tsp ground ginger
- ½ tsp turmeric
- 1 cup chicken broth
- 1 cup canned chickpeas, drained and rinsed
- 1 preserved lemon, flesh discarded and rind sliced
- ½ cup green olives, pitted and halved
- Fresh cilantro or parsley for garnish
- Salt and pepper to taste

Instructions:

1. In a large skillet or tagine pot, heat olive oil over medium heat and add chopped onion, cooking until soft and translucent.
2. Add the garlic and spices (cumin, coriander, cinnamon, ginger, turmeric) and sauté for another minute until fragrant.
3. Add the chicken thighs, browning them on all sides, then pour in the chicken broth, and bring to a simmer.
4. Stir in the chickpeas, preserved lemon, and olives, cover, and let it cook on low heat for about 40 minutes, or until the chicken is tender and cooked through.
5. Serve the tagine garnished with fresh cilantro or parsley, accompanied by couscous or whole grain bread to soak up the sauce.

Nutritional Information (per serving):

- *Calories:* 380
- *Protein:* 28g
- *Carbohydrates:* 30g
- *Fats:* 18g
- *Fiber:* 8g
- *Cholesterol:* 90mg
- *Sodium:* 600mg
- *Potassium:* 700mg

Roasted Red Pepper Chicken Thighs

Yield: *4 servings*
Preparation Time: *15 minutes*
Cooking Time: *40 minutes*

Ingredients:

- **For the Chicken:**

    o 4 boneless, skinless chicken thighs (about 6 oz each)
    o 2 tbsp olive oil
    o 1 cup roasted red peppers, jarred or homemade, chopped
    o 2 cloves garlic, minced
    o 1 tsp dried oregano
    o 1 tsp smoked paprika
    o Salt and pepper to taste
    o Fresh basil or parsley for garnish

Instructions:

1. Preheat the oven to 400°F (200°C) and grease a baking dish with olive oil. In a bowl, combine the chopped roasted red peppers, minced garlic, oregano, smoked paprika, salt, and pepper to create a sauce.
2. Place the chicken thighs in the baking dish and pour the roasted red pepper sauce over them, ensuring they are well coated.
3. Bake for 30-35 minutes until the chicken is cooked through and has reached an internal temperature of 165°F (75°C).
4. Remove from the oven and let rest for 5 minutes before serving to retain moisture.
5. Serve the chicken thighs over a bed of quinoa or brown rice, garnished with fresh basil or parsley.

Nutritional Information (per serving):
- *Calories: 320*
- *Protein: 30g*
- *Carbohydrates: 12g*
- *Fats: 18g*
- *Fiber: 3g*
- *Cholesterol: 95mg*
- *Sodium: 500mg*
- *Potassium: 550mg*

Stuffed Chicken Breast with Spinach and Feta

Yield: *4 servings*
Preparation Time: *15 minutes*
Cooking Time: *30 minutes*

Ingredients:

- **For the Chicken:**

    o 4 boneless, skinless chicken breasts (about 6 oz each)
    o 2 cups fresh spinach, chopped
    o 1 cup feta cheese, crumbled
    o 2 cloves garlic, minced
    o 1 tbsp olive oil
    o 1 tsp dried oregano
    o Salt and pepper to taste

Instructions:

1. Preheat the oven to 375°F (190°C) and lightly grease a baking dish. In a skillet, heat olive oil over medium heat and sauté the garlic until fragrant, then add the chopped spinach and cook until wilted; remove from heat and stir in feta cheese and oregano, seasoning with salt and pepper.
2. Using a sharp knife, create a pocket in each chicken breast by slicing it horizontally, being careful not to cut all the way through.
3. Stuff each chicken breast with the spinach and feta mixture, securing the opening with toothpicks if needed, and season the outside with salt and pepper.
4. Place the stuffed chicken breasts in the baking dish and bake for 25-30 minutes, or until the chicken is cooked through and reaches an internal temperature of 165°F (75°C).
5. Allow to rest for a few minutes before serving, with lemon wedges on the side for added flavor.

Nutritional Information (per serving):
- *Calories: 290*
- *Protein: 36g*
- *Carbohydrates: 3g*
- *Fats: 15g*
- *Fiber: 1g*
- *Cholesterol: 90mg*
- *Sodium: 500mg*
- *Potassium: 450mg*

Chicken Gyro with Tzatziki Sauce

Yield: *4 servings*
Preparation Time: *15 minutes*
Cooking Time: *20 minutes*

Ingredients:

- **For the Chicken:**
  - 1 lb boneless, skinless chicken breasts, thinly sliced
  - 3 tbsp olive oil
  - 2 tsp dried oregano
  - 1 tsp garlic powder
  - 1 tsp paprika
  - Salt and pepper to taste
  - 4 whole wheat pita bread
- **For the Tzatziki Sauce:**
  - 1 cup plain Greek yogurt
  - 1 cucumber, grated and drained
  - 2 cloves garlic, minced
  - 1 tbsp fresh dill (or 1 tsp dried dill)
  - 1 tbsp lemon juice
  - Salt to taste
- **For Serving:**
  - Sliced tomatoes
  - Shredded lettuce
  - Red onion, thinly sliced

Instructions:

1. In a bowl, combine the olive oil, oregano, garlic powder, paprika, salt, and pepper; add the chicken slices and marinate for at least 10 minutes.
2. While the chicken marinates, prepare the tzatziki sauce by mixing the Greek yogurt, grated cucumber, minced garlic, dill, lemon juice, and salt in a bowl; refrigerate until ready to serve.
3. Heat a skillet over medium-high heat and cook the marinated chicken for about 5-7 minutes, or until cooked through and golden brown.
4. Warm the pita bread in a separate pan or oven, then fill each pita with the cooked chicken, tomatoes, lettuce, and red onion.
5. Drizzle tzatziki sauce over the filling and fold the pita; serve immediately with extra sauce on the side.

Nutritional Information (per serving):

- **Calories:** *400*
- **Protein:** *32g*
- **Carbohydrates:** *40g*
- **Fats:** *12g*
- **Fiber:** *5g*
- **Cholesterol:** *80mg*
- **Sodium:** *600mg*
- **Potassium:** *600mg*

Lemon and Rosemary Grilled Chicken

Yield: *4 servings*
Preparation Time: *15 minutes*
Marinating Time: *30 minutes*
Cooking Time: *15 minutes*

Ingredients:

- **For the Chicken:**
  - 4 boneless, skinless chicken breasts (about 6 oz each)
  - 4 tbsp extra virgin olive oil
  - 2 lemons (zested and juiced)
  - 2 tbsp fresh rosemary, chopped (or 1 tbsp dried rosemary)
  - 3 cloves garlic, minced
  - Salt and pepper to taste
- **For Serving (optional):**
  - Fresh salad (e.g., mixed greens, tomatoes, cucumber)
  - Quinoa or whole grain couscous

Instructions:

1. In a bowl, whisk together olive oil, lemon juice, lemon zest, rosemary, garlic, salt, and pepper; add the chicken breasts and marinate for at least 30 minutes.
2. Preheat the grill to medium-high heat and lightly oil the grates to prevent sticking.
3. Remove the chicken from the marinade and grill for about 6-7 minutes on each side, or until the internal temperature reaches 165°F (75°C).
4. Let the chicken rest for a few minutes after grilling before slicing.
5. Serve the chicken over a bed of fresh salad or alongside quinoa, drizzling any remaining marinade over the top for added flavor.

Nutritional Information (per serving):
- **Calories:** *290*
- **Protein:** *30g*
- **Carbohydrates:** *2g*
- **Fats:** *18g*
- **Fiber:** *0g*
- **Cholesterol:** *90mg*
- **Sodium:** *450mg*
- **Potassium:** *400mg*

Olive Oil Roasted Chicken with Fresh Thyme

Yield: *4 servings*
Preparation Time: *15 minutes*
Cooking Time: *1 hour*

Ingredients:

- **For the Chicken:**
  - 4 bone-in, skin-on chicken thighs (about 6 oz each)
  - 4 tbsp extra virgin olive oil
  - 2 tbsp fresh thyme leaves (or 1 tbsp dried thyme)
  - 4 cloves garlic, minced
  - 1 lemon, zested and juiced
  - Salt and pepper to taste
  - 1 tsp paprika (optional)

Instructions:

1. Preheat the oven to 425°F (220°C) and lightly grease a baking dish. In a bowl, mix olive oil, minced garlic, lemon juice, lemon zest, thyme, salt, pepper, and paprika.
2. Rub the chicken thighs with the olive oil mixture, ensuring they are well coated, and place them skin-side up in the prepared baking dish.
3. Roast in the preheated oven for 45-50 minutes, or until the chicken reaches an internal temperature of 165°F (75°C) and the skin is crispy.
4. During the last 10 minutes, add any desired vegetables to the baking dish for roasting alongside the chicken, drizzling them with olive oil and seasoning.
5. Let the chicken rest for a few minutes before serving, garnished with additional fresh thyme if desired.

Nutritional Information (per serving):
- **Calories:** *360*
- **Protein:** *28g*
- **Carbohydrates:** *2g*
- **Fats:** *26g*
- **Fiber:** *0g*
- **Cholesterol:** *130mg*
- **Sodium:** *450mg*
- **Potassium:** *380mg*

CHAPTER 8: MEAT RECIPES

Grilled Lamb Chops with Mint and Lemon

Yield: *4 servings*
Preparation Time: *15 minutes*
Marinating Time: *1 hour*
Cooking Time: *10 minutes*

Ingredients:

- **For the Lamb Chops:**
    - 8 lamb chops (about 1 inch thick)
    - 1/4 cup extra virgin olive oil
    - 2 lemons (zested and juiced)
    - 3 tbsp fresh mint, chopped (or 1 tbsp dried mint)
    - 3 cloves garlic, minced
    - Salt and pepper to taste

Instructions:

1. In a bowl, whisk together olive oil, lemon juice, lemon zest, mint, garlic, salt, and pepper; add lamb chops and marinate for at least 1 hour in the refrigerator.
2. Preheat the grill to medium-high heat and lightly oil the grates to prevent sticking.
3. Remove the lamb chops from the marinade, letting excess marinade drip off, and grill for about 4-5 minutes per side for medium-rare, or until the internal temperature reaches 145°F (63°C).
4. Remove the chops from the grill and let them rest for 5 minutes before serving.
5. Serve the lamb chops with a side of grilled vegetables or a fresh salad drizzled with olive oil and lemon for added Mediterranean flair.

Nutritional Information (per serving):
- **Calories:** *320*
- **Protein:** *25g*
- **Carbohydrates:** *3g*
- **Fats:** *24g*
- **Fiber:** *0g*
- **Cholesterol:** *75mg*
- **Sodium:** *420mg*
- **Potassium:** *380mg*

Mediterranean Beef Kabobs with Tzatziki

Yield: 4 servings
Preparation Time: 20 minutes
Marinating Time: 30 minutes
Cooking Time: 15 minutes

Ingredients:

- **For the Beef Kabobs:**
  - 1.5 lbs beef sirloin, cut into 1-inch cubes
  - 1/4 cup extra virgin olive oil
  - 2 tbsp red wine vinegar
  - 3 cloves garlic, minced
  - 2 tsp dried oregano
  - 1 tsp ground cumin
  - Salt and pepper to taste
  - 1 red bell pepper, cut into squares
  - 1 yellow bell pepper, cut into squares
  - 1 red onion, cut into wedges
  - Skewers (soaked in water if wooden)
- **For the Tzatziki Sauce:**
  - 1 cup Greek yogurt
  - 1 cucumber, grated and excess water squeezed out
  - 2 cloves garlic, minced
  - 1 tbsp olive oil
  - 1 tbsp fresh dill, chopped (or 1 tsp dried dill)
  - Juice of 1/2 lemon
  - Salt to taste

Instructions:

1. In a large bowl, whisk together olive oil, red wine vinegar, garlic, oregano, cumin, salt, and pepper; add the beef cubes and marinate for at least 30 minutes.
2. Preheat a grill or grill pan to medium-high heat, and thread the marinated beef, bell peppers, and onion onto the skewers.
3. Grill the kabobs for about 10-15 minutes, turning occasionally, until the beef is cooked to your desired doneness (medium-rare at 135°F or 57°C).
4. For the tzatziki sauce, combine Greek yogurt, grated cucumber, garlic, olive oil, dill, lemon juice, and salt in a bowl; mix well and refrigerate until serving.
5. Serve the beef kabobs hot with tzatziki sauce on the side, accompanied by whole grain pita or a Greek salad for a complete Mediterranean meal.

Nutritional Information (per serving):

- *Calories: 400*
- *Protein: 32g*
- *Carbohydrates: 10g*
- *Fats: 25g*
- *Fiber: 1g*
- *Cholesterol: 85mg*
- *Sodium: 550mg*
- *Potassium: 700mg*

Moroccan Lamb Tagine with Apricots

Yield: 4 servings
Preparation Time: 15 minutes
Cooking Time: 1 hour 30 minutes

Ingredients:

- 1.5 lbs lamb shoulder, cut into 1.5-inch cubes
- 2 tbsp olive oil
- 1 large onion, finely chopped
- 3 cloves garlic, minced
- 2 tsp ground cumin
- 1 tsp ground cinnamon
- 1 tsp ground ginger
- 1/2 tsp ground turmeric
- 1/2 tsp cayenne pepper (adjust for spice level)
- Salt and pepper to taste
- 1 can (14 oz) diced tomatoes, drained
- 1.5 cups chicken or vegetable broth
- 1 cup dried apricots, halved
- 1/4 cup almonds, toasted
- Fresh cilantro or parsley for garnish (optional)

Instructions:

1. In a large pot or tagine, heat olive oil over medium heat and sauté the onions until translucent; add garlic and spices (cumin, cinnamon, ginger, turmeric, cayenne, salt, and pepper) and cook for 1-2 minutes until fragrant.
2. Add the lamb cubes to the pot, browning on all sides for about 5-7 minutes.
3. Stir in the diced tomatoes and broth, bringing to a boil; reduce heat, cover, and simmer for about 1 hour, until the lamb is tender.
4. Add the dried apricots and simmer uncovered for an additional 15 minutes to allow flavors to meld and sauce to thicken.
5. Serve the tagine hot, garnished with toasted almonds and fresh herbs, over couscous or with whole grain bread for a complete meal.

Nutritional Information (per serving):

- **Calories:** 480
- **Protein:** 35g
- **Carbohydrates:** 45g
- **Fats:** 22g
- **Fiber:** 4g
- **Cholesterol:** 95mg
- **Sodium:** 500mg
- **Potassium:** 800mg

Beef and Vegetable Moussaka

Yield: *6 servings*
Preparation Time: *30 minutes*
Cooking Time: *1 hour*

Ingredients:

- **For the meat sauce:**
    - 1 lb lean ground beef or lamb
    - 1 medium onion, finely chopped
    - 2 cloves garlic, minced
    - 1 can (14 oz) diced tomatoes, drained
    - 1 tsp dried oregano
    - 1 tsp ground cinnamon
    - Salt and pepper to taste
- **For the vegetable layers:**
    - 2 medium eggplants, sliced into 1/2-inch rounds
    - 2 medium zucchini, sliced into 1/4-inch rounds
    - 1 medium bell pepper, chopped
    - 2 tbsp olive oil
    - Salt and pepper to taste
- **For the béchamel sauce:**
    - 2 tbsp olive oil
    - 2 tbsp all-purpose flour
    - 2 cups low-fat milk
    - 1/2 cup grated Parmesan cheese
    - 1/4 tsp nutmeg
    - Salt and pepper to taste

Instructions:

1. Preheat the oven to 375°F (190°C) and salt the eggplant slices; let them sit for 15 minutes to draw out moisture, then rinse and pat dry.
2. In a skillet, heat 1 tbsp olive oil, sauté onion and garlic until soft, add the ground meat, cooking until browned; stir in tomatoes, oregano, cinnamon, salt, and pepper, simmer for 10 minutes.
3. In another skillet, heat 1 tbsp olive oil and sauté zucchini, bell pepper, and eggplant until slightly softened, about 5-7 minutes; season with salt and pepper.
4. For the béchamel sauce, heat 2 tbsp olive oil, whisk in flour until golden, gradually add milk, stirring until thickened, then stir in cheese, nutmeg, salt, and pepper.
5. In a baking dish, layer half of the sautéed vegetables, followed by the meat sauce, remaining vegetables, and pour béchamel on top; bake for 30-35 minutes until golden.

Nutritional Information (per serving):
- **Calories:** *360*
- **Protein:** *28g*
- **Carbohydrates:** *26g*
- **Fats:** *18g*
- **Fiber:** *5g*
- **Cholesterol:** *60mg*
- **Sodium:** *450mg*
- **Potassium:** *700mg*

Garlic and Herb Crusted Pork Tenderloin

Yield: 4 servings
Preparation Time: 15 minutes
Cooking Time: 25 minutes

Ingredients:

- 1 lb pork tenderloin
- 3 cloves garlic, minced
- 2 tbsp fresh rosemary, chopped (or 1 tbsp dried)
- 2 tbsp fresh thyme, chopped (or 1 tbsp dried)
- 2 tbsp Dijon mustard
- 2 tbsp olive oil
- Salt and pepper to taste

Instructions:

1. Preheat the oven to 400°F (200°C) and line a baking dish with parchment paper.
2. In a bowl, combine minced garlic, rosemary, thyme, Dijon mustard, olive oil, salt, and pepper to create a paste.
3. Rub the garlic and herb mixture all over the pork tenderloin, ensuring it's evenly coated.
4. Place the pork in the prepared baking dish and roast for 20-25 minutes, or until the internal temperature reaches 145°F (63°C).
5. Let the pork rest for 5 minutes before slicing and serving.

Nutritional Information (per serving):

- *Calories:* 240
- *Protein:* 28g
- *Carbohydrates:* 2g
- *Fats:* 13g
- *Fiber:* 0g
- *Cholesterol:* 80mg
- *Sodium:* 500mg
- *Potassium:* 500mg

Braised Beef with Olives and Tomatoes

Yield: 4 servings
Preparation Time: 15 minutes
Cooking Time: 2 hours

Ingredients:

- 2 lbs beef chuck roast, cut into 1.5-inch cubes
- 2 tbsp olive oil
- 1 medium onion, finely chopped
- 3 cloves garlic, minced
- 1 can (14 oz) diced tomatoes (with juices)
- 1 cup beef broth
- 1/2 cup green olives, pitted and halved
- 1 tsp dried oregano
- 1 tsp dried thyme
- Salt and pepper to taste
- Fresh parsley, chopped (for garnish)

Instructions:

1. Heat olive oil in a large Dutch oven over medium-high heat; season beef with salt and pepper, then brown the meat on all sides (about 5-7 minutes).
2. Remove the beef and add onion and garlic to the pot, sautéing until softened (about 3 minutes).
3. Return the beef to the pot, then stir in the diced tomatoes, beef broth, olives, oregano, and thyme; bring to a simmer.
4. Cover and braise in a preheated oven at 325°F (165°C) for about 1.5 hours, or until the beef is tender.
5. Serve hot, garnished with fresh parsley, alongside whole grain couscous or a mixed green salad.

Nutritional Information (per serving):
- *Calories:* 400
- *Protein:* 36g
- *Carbohydrates:* 10g
- *Fats:* 25g
- *Fiber:* 2g
- *Cholesterol:* 90mg
- *Sodium:* 600mg
- *Potassium:* 700mg

Spicy Lamb Meatballs with Yogurt Sauce

Yield: *4 servings*
Preparation Time: *15 minutes*
Cooking Time: *20 minutes*

Ingredients:

For the Meatballs:

- 1 lb ground lamb
- 1/4 cup breadcrumbs (whole wheat preferred)
- 1/4 cup fresh parsley, chopped
- 2 cloves garlic, minced
- 1 tsp cumin
- 1 tsp smoked paprika
- 1/2 tsp cayenne pepper (adjust to taste)
- Salt and pepper to taste
- 1 egg, beaten

For the Yogurt Sauce:

- 1 cup plain Greek yogurt
- 1 tbsp olive oil
- 1 clove garlic, minced
- 1 tbsp lemon juice
- Salt to taste
- Fresh mint leaves, chopped (optional, for garnish)

Instructions:

1. Preheat the oven to 400°F (200°C) and line a baking sheet with parchment paper.
2. In a large bowl, combine the ground lamb, breadcrumbs, parsley, garlic, spices, salt, pepper, and beaten egg; mix until well combined.
3. Form the mixture into small meatballs (about 1 inch in diameter) and place them on the prepared baking sheet.
4. Bake for 15-20 minutes, or until cooked through and browned, while mixing the yogurt sauce by combining Greek yogurt, olive oil, minced garlic, lemon juice, and salt in a bowl.
5. Serve the meatballs warm, drizzled with the yogurt sauce and garnished with fresh mint if desired.

Nutritional Information (per serving):

- *Calories: 320*
- *Protein: 24g*
- *Carbohydrates: 12g*
- *Fats: 20g*
- *Fiber: 1g*
- *Cholesterol: 90mg*
- *Sodium: 450mg*
- *Potassium: 450mg*

Beef Shawarma with Garlic Sauce

Yield: *4 servings*
Preparation Time: *15 minutes*
Marinating Time: *1-2 hours (or overnight)*
Cooking Time: *15 minutes*

Ingredients:

For the Beef Shawarma:

- 1 lb flank steak or sirloin, thinly sliced
- 3 tbsp olive oil
- 2 tsp ground cumin
- 2 tsp ground coriander
- 1 tsp ground paprika
- 1 tsp ground turmeric
- 1/2 tsp ground cinnamon
- 1/2 tsp cayenne pepper (adjust to taste)
- Salt and pepper to taste
- Juice of 1 lemon
- 2 cloves garlic, minced

For the Garlic Sauce:

- 1 cup plain Greek yogurt
- 2 tbsp tahini
- 3 cloves garlic, minced
- 2 tbsp lemon juice
- Salt to taste

Instructions:

1. In a large bowl, mix olive oil, spices, lemon juice, and minced garlic; add the sliced beef and marinate for at least 1 hour.
2. Heat a skillet or grill over medium-high heat; cook the marinated beef for 8-10 minutes, stirring occasionally until browned and cooked through.
3. While the beef is cooking, combine Greek yogurt, tahini, garlic, lemon juice, and salt in a separate bowl to make the garlic sauce.
4. Serve the beef in whole wheat pita bread or over a bed of lettuce with sliced cucumbers and tomatoes, drizzling with garlic sauce.
5. Garnish with fresh parsley or mint for extra flavor, if desired.

Nutritional Information (per serving):
- *Calories: 380*
- *Protein: 32g*
- *Carbohydrates: 20g*
- *Fats: 20g*
- *Fiber: 3g*
- *Cholesterol: 90mg*
- *Sodium: 600mg*
- *Potassium: 600mg*

Mediterranean Stuffed Bell Peppers with Lamb

Yield: *4 servings*
Preparation Time: *15 minutes*
Cooking Time: *30 minutes*

Ingredients:
- 4 large bell peppers (any color)
- 1 lb ground lamb
- 1 cup cooked quinoa (or brown rice)
- 1 medium onion, finely chopped
- 2 cloves garlic, minced
- 1 can (14 oz) diced tomatoes (drained)
- 1 tsp dried oregano
- 1 tsp ground cumin
- 1/2 tsp paprika
- Salt and pepper to taste
- 1/4 cup fresh parsley, chopped (for garnish)
- 1/2 cup feta cheese, crumbled (optional)

Instructions:
1. Preheat the oven to 375°F (190°C). Cut the tops off the bell peppers and remove the seeds, placing them upright in a baking dish.
2. In a skillet over medium heat, sauté the onion and garlic until softened (about 3-4 minutes), then add the ground lamb and cook until browned (about 5-7 minutes).
3. Stir in the cooked quinoa, diced tomatoes, oregano, cumin, paprika, salt, and pepper, cooking for another 2 minutes to combine flavors.
4. Stuff each bell pepper with the lamb mixture, then cover the dish with aluminum foil and bake for 25 minutes.
5. Remove the foil, sprinkle with feta cheese (if using), and bake for an additional 5 minutes until the peppers are tender and the filling is heated through.

Nutritional Information (per serving):
- **Calories:** *320*
- **Protein:** *25g*
- **Carbohydrates:** *30g*
- **Fats:** *15g*
- **Fiber:** *5g*
- **Cholesterol:** *70mg*
- **Sodium:** *300mg*
- **Potassium:** *600mg*

Herb-Marinated Grilled Steak

Yield: *4 servings*
Preparation Time: *15 minutes (plus 1 hour marinating)*
Cooking Time: *10 minutes*

Ingredients:
- 1 lb flank steak (or sirloin)
- 1/4 cup extra virgin olive oil
- 3 cloves garlic, minced
- 2 tbsp fresh rosemary, chopped (or 1 tbsp dried)
- 2 tbsp fresh thyme, chopped (or 1 tbsp dried)
- 1 tsp salt
- 1/2 tsp black pepper
- Juice of 1 lemon
- Optional: Red pepper flakes for added heat

Instructions:
1. In a bowl, mix olive oil, garlic, rosemary, thyme, salt, pepper, lemon juice, and optional red pepper flakes to create the marinade.
2. Place the steak in a resealable plastic bag or shallow dish and pour the marinade over it, ensuring it's well coated; marinate for at least 1 hour in the refrigerator.
3. Preheat the grill to medium-high heat and remove the steak from the marinade, letting excess drip off.
4. Grill the steak for about 5 minutes per side (for medium-rare), or until desired doneness is reached, using a meat thermometer to check (130°F for medium-rare).
5. Let the steak rest for 5 minutes before slicing against the grain and serving.

Nutritional Information (per serving):
- **Calories:** *320*
- **Protein:** *30g*
- **Carbohydrates:** *2g*
- **Fats:** *22g*
- **Fiber:** *0g*
- **Cholesterol:** *80mg*
- **Sodium:** *320mg*
- **Potassium:** *450mg*

Pork Souvlaki with Lemon Potatoes

Yield: 4 servings
Preparation Time: 20 minutes (plus 1 hour marinating)
Cooking Time: 30 minutes

Ingredients:

For the Pork Souvlaki:

- 1 lb pork tenderloin, cut into 1-inch cubes
- 1/4 cup extra virgin olive oil
- 3 cloves garlic, minced
- 2 tbsp fresh oregano, chopped (or 1 tbsp dried)
- Juice of 1 lemon
- 1 tsp salt
- 1/2 tsp black pepper
- Wooden skewers (soaked in water for 30 minutes)

For the Lemon Potatoes:

- 1.5 lbs baby potatoes, halved
- 1/4 cup extra virgin olive oil
- Juice of 1 lemon
- 2 tsp dried oregano
- 1 tsp salt
- 1/2 tsp black pepper
- 1 cup chicken or vegetable broth

Instructions:

1. In a bowl, mix olive oil, garlic, oregano, lemon juice, salt, and pepper; add pork cubes and marinate for at least 1 hour in the refrigerator.
2. Preheat the oven to 400°F (200°C) for the potatoes and soak skewers in water while the pork marinates.
3. Toss the halved baby potatoes with olive oil, lemon juice, oregano, salt, and pepper in a baking dish; pour broth around the potatoes and bake for 30 minutes, or until tender.
4. Thread marinated pork onto soaked skewers and grill over medium-high heat for about 10-12 minutes, turning occasionally until cooked through (145°F internal temperature).
5. Serve the pork souvlaki with the lemon potatoes and garnish with additional lemon wedges and fresh herbs.

Nutritional Information (per serving):

- *Calories: 480*
- *Protein: 30g*
- *Carbohydrates: 40g*
- *Fats: 25g*
- *Fiber: 4g*
- *Cholesterol: 75mg*
- *Sodium: 500mg*
- *Potassium: 850mg*

Balsamic Glazed Lamb Chops

Yield: *4 servings*
Preparation Time: *15 minutes*
Cooking Time: *15 minutes*

Ingredients:

- 8 lamb chops (about 1 inch thick)
- 1/2 cup balsamic vinegar
- 2 tablespoons honey or maple syrup
- 2 tablespoons olive oil
- 3 cloves garlic, minced
- 1 teaspoon fresh rosemary, chopped (or 1/2 teaspoon dried)
- 1 teaspoon fresh thyme, chopped (or 1/2 teaspoon dried)
- Salt and pepper to taste

Instructions:

1. In a small bowl, whisk together balsamic vinegar, honey, olive oil, garlic, rosemary, thyme, salt, and pepper to create the glaze.
2. Heat a skillet over medium-high heat and add lamb chops, searing for 3-4 minutes on each side until browned.
3. Reduce heat to medium, pour the balsamic glaze over the lamb, and cook for an additional 3-5 minutes, turning to coat.
4. Remove the lamb chops from the skillet and let them rest for 5 minutes to allow flavors to meld.
5. Serve with a side of roasted vegetables or a fresh Mediterranean salad.

Nutritional Information (per serving):

- *Calories: 350*
- *Protein: 28g*
- *Carbohydrates: 14g*
- *Fats: 20g*
- *Fiber: 0g*
- *Cholesterol: 85mg*
- *Sodium: 320mg*
- *Potassium: 500mg*

Beef and Tomato Stew with Fresh Herbs

Yield: *4 servings*
Preparation Time: *15 minutes*
Cooking Time: *1 hour 30 minutes*

Ingredients:

- 1.5 lbs lean beef chuck, cut into 1-inch cubes
- 2 tablespoons olive oil
- 1 onion, chopped
- 3 cloves garlic, minced
- 4 large tomatoes, diced (or one 28 oz can of diced tomatoes)
- 2 cups beef broth (low-sodium)
- 1 teaspoon dried oregano
- 1 teaspoon dried basil
- 1 teaspoon fresh parsley, chopped (or 1/2 teaspoon dried)
- Salt and pepper to taste

Instructions:

1. In a large pot, heat olive oil over medium-high heat and brown the beef cubes on all sides, about 5-7 minutes.
2. Add the onion and garlic, cooking until softened, about 5 minutes.
3. Stir in the tomatoes, beef broth, oregano, basil, salt, and pepper; bring to a boil.
4. Reduce heat to low, cover, and simmer for about 1 hour, stirring occasionally, until the beef is tender.
5. Stir in fresh parsley before serving; enjoy with whole grain bread or over brown rice.

Nutritional Information (per serving):

- *Calories: 320*
- *Protein: 28g*
- *Carbohydrates: 14g*
- *Fats: 15g*
- *Fiber: 3g*
- *Cholesterol: 70mg*
- *Sodium: 300mg*
- *Potassium: 650mg*

Lamb Kofte with Fresh Mint and Parsley

Yield: *4 servings*
Preparation Time: *15 minutes*
Cooking Time: *10 minutes*

Ingredients:

- 1 lb ground lamb (or lean beef)
- 1/4 cup fresh mint, finely chopped
- 1/4 cup fresh parsley, finely chopped
- 2 cloves garlic, minced
- 1 teaspoon ground cumin
- 1 teaspoon paprika
- 1/2 teaspoon salt
- 1/4 teaspoon black pepper
- 1 tablespoon olive oil (for grilling)

Instructions:

1. In a large bowl, combine ground lamb, mint, parsley, garlic, cumin, paprika, salt, and pepper; mix well until combined.
2. Form the mixture into elongated patties or meatballs (about 2 inches long).
3. Heat olive oil in a skillet over medium-high heat, then add the koftes, cooking for 4-5 minutes on each side until browned and cooked through.
4. Remove from the skillet and let rest for a few minutes to retain moisture.
5. Serve with whole grain pita and a side of tzatziki sauce or a fresh salad.

Nutritional Information (per serving):

- *Calories: 280*
- *Protein: 22g*
- *Carbohydrates: 3g*
- *Fats: 20g*
- *Fiber: 0g*
- *Cholesterol: 80mg*
- *Sodium: 300mg*
- *Potassium: 350mg*

Beef and Spinach Stuffed Zucchini

Yield: *4 servings*
Preparation Time: *15 minutes*
Cooking Time: *30 minutes*

Ingredients:

- 4 medium zucchinis
- 1 lb lean ground beef
- 2 cups fresh spinach, chopped
- 1/2 cup onion, diced
- 2 cloves garlic, minced
- 1 cup diced tomatoes (fresh or canned)
- 1 teaspoon dried oregano
- 1 teaspoon dried basil
- 1/2 teaspoon salt
- 1/4 teaspoon black pepper
- 1/2 cup feta cheese, crumbled (optional)

Instructions:

1. Preheat the oven to 375°F (190°C) and slice the zucchinis in half lengthwise; scoop out the seeds to create boats.
2. In a skillet, heat olive oil over medium heat, sauté onions and garlic until soft, then add ground beef and cook until browned.
3. Stir in spinach, diced tomatoes, oregano, basil, salt, and pepper, cooking for an additional 3-4 minutes until spinach wilts.
4. Fill each zucchini half with the beef mixture and place them in a baking dish; sprinkle feta cheese on top if using.
5. Bake for 20 minutes, until zucchinis are tender; serve warm.

Nutritional Information (per serving):

- *Calories: 280*
- *Protein: 25g*
- *Carbohydrates: 10g*
- *Fats: 15g*
- *Fiber: 3g*
- *Cholesterol: 70mg*
- *Sodium: 300mg*
- *Potassium: 700mg*

Garlic Roasted Pork Shoulder

Yield: 6 servings
Preparation Time: 15 minutes
Cooking Time: 3 hours

Ingredients:

- 3 lbs pork shoulder (bone-in or boneless)
- 10 cloves garlic, minced
- 1/4 cup olive oil
- 2 tablespoons fresh rosemary, chopped (or 2 teaspoons dried)
- 1 tablespoon fresh thyme, chopped (or 1 teaspoon dried)
- 1 teaspoon salt
- 1/2 teaspoon black pepper
- 1 cup low-sodium chicken broth
- Zest of 1 lemon

Instructions:

1. Preheat the oven to 300°F (150°C); in a bowl, mix garlic, olive oil, rosemary, thyme, salt, pepper, and lemon zest to create a marinade.
2. Rub the marinade all over the pork shoulder, ensuring it is well coated; place it in a roasting pan.
3. Pour chicken broth into the pan and cover with foil; roast in the oven for 2.5 hours.
4. Remove the foil and increase the oven temperature to 425°F (220°C), roasting for an additional 30 minutes until the skin is crispy and the meat is tender.
5. Let the pork rest for 10-15 minutes before slicing; serve with roasted vegetables or a fresh salad.

Nutritional Information (per serving):

- *Calories:* 380
- *Protein:* 30g
- *Carbohydrates:* 1g
- *Fats:* 28g
- *Fiber:* 0g
- *Cholesterol:* 90mg
- *Sodium:* 250mg
- *Potassium:* 650mg

CHAPTER 9: VEGETABLE RECIPES

Roasted Eggplant with Tahini and Pomegranate

Yield: 4 servings
Preparation Time: 10 minutes
Cooking Time: 30 minutes

Ingredients:
- 2 medium eggplants
- 1/4 cup olive oil
- 1/2 teaspoon salt
- 1/4 teaspoon black pepper
- 1/3 cup tahini
- 2 tablespoons lemon juice
- 1 tablespoon honey or maple syrup (optional)
- 1/2 cup pomegranate seeds
- Fresh parsley, chopped (for garnish)

Instructions:
1. Preheat the oven to 400°F (200°C) and slice the eggplants in half lengthwise; score the flesh with a knife and brush with olive oil, then season with salt and pepper.
2. Place the eggplant halves cut side down on a baking sheet and roast for 25-30 minutes, until tender and golden.
3. In a small bowl, whisk together tahini, lemon juice, and honey (if using) until smooth; add a little water to thin if necessary.
4. Once the eggplants are done, flip them cut side up, drizzle with tahini sauce, and sprinkle with pomegranate seeds.
5. Garnish with fresh parsley and serve warm or at room temperature.

Nutritional Information (per serving):
- *Calories:* 220
- *Protein:* 5g
- *Carbohydrates:* 18g
- *Fats:* 16g
- *Fiber:* 7g
- *Cholesterol:* 0mg
- *Sodium:* 200mg
- *Potassium:* 650mg

Stuffed Bell Peppers with Quinoa and Feta

Yield: 4 servings
Preparation Time: 15 minutes
Cooking Time: 30 minutes

Ingredients:
- 4 large bell peppers (any color)
- 1 cup cooked quinoa
- 1 cup diced tomatoes (fresh or canned)
- 1/2 cup feta cheese, crumbled
- 1/2 cup black olives, sliced (optional)
- 1/4 cup fresh parsley, chopped
- 1 teaspoon dried oregano
- 1 teaspoon olive oil
- Salt and pepper to taste

Instructions:
1. Preheat the oven to 375°F (190°C) and cut the tops off the bell peppers, removing seeds and membranes.
2. In a bowl, combine cooked quinoa, diced tomatoes, feta cheese, olives, parsley, oregano, olive oil, salt, and pepper.
3. Stuff each bell pepper with the quinoa mixture, packing it in gently.
4. Place the stuffed peppers upright in a baking dish and add a splash of water to the bottom to create steam; cover with foil.
5. Bake for 25-30 minutes until peppers are tender; serve warm, garnished with additional parsley if desired.

Nutritional Information (per serving):
- *Calories:* 240
- *Protein:* 9g
- *Carbohydrates:* 30g
- *Fats:* 10g
- *Fiber:* 6g
- *Cholesterol:* 20mg
- *Sodium:* 300mg
- *Potassium:* 500mg

Ratatouille with Fresh Herbs

Yield: 4 servings
Preparation Time: 15 minutes
Cooking Time: 35 minutes

Ingredients:

- 1 medium eggplant, diced
- 2 medium zucchinis, sliced
- 1 bell pepper, chopped
- 1 medium onion, chopped
- 2 cups diced tomatoes (fresh or canned)
- 3 cloves garlic, minced
- 1/4 cup olive oil
- 1 teaspoon dried thyme
- 1 teaspoon dried basil
- Salt and pepper to taste
- Fresh basil and parsley for garnish

Instructions:

1. In a large skillet or pot, heat olive oil over medium heat and sauté onion and garlic until softened, about 5 minutes.
2. Add eggplant, bell pepper, and zucchini; cook for another 10 minutes until vegetables begin to soften.
3. Stir in diced tomatoes, thyme, basil, salt, and pepper; simmer uncovered for 15-20 minutes, stirring occasionally.
4. Adjust seasoning if needed, and let it cool slightly to allow flavors to meld.
5. Serve warm, garnished with fresh basil and parsley.

Nutritional Information (per serving):
- *Calories:* 180
- *Protein:* 4g
- *Carbohydrates:* 15g
- *Fats:* 12g
- *Fiber:* 5g
- *Cholesterol:* 0mg
- *Sodium:* 200mg
- *Potassium:* 600mg

Mediterranean Roasted Cauliflower with Cumin

Yield: 4 servings
Preparation Time: 10 minutes
Cooking Time: 25 minutes

Ingredients:

- 1 large head of cauliflower, cut into florets
- 3 tablespoons olive oil
- 2 teaspoons ground cumin
- 1 teaspoon smoked paprika
- 1/2 teaspoon salt
- 1/4 teaspoon black pepper
- Juice of 1 lemon
- Fresh parsley, chopped (for garnish)

Instructions:

1. Preheat the oven to 425°F (220°C) and line a baking sheet with parchment paper.
2. In a large bowl, toss cauliflower florets with olive oil, cumin, smoked paprika, salt, and pepper until well coated.
3. Spread the seasoned cauliflower on the prepared baking sheet in a single layer.
4. Roast for 20-25 minutes, stirring halfway through, until cauliflower is golden and tender.
5. Drizzle with lemon juice and garnish with fresh parsley before serving.

Nutritional Information (per serving):
- *Calories:* 150
- *Protein:* 4g
- *Carbohydrates:* 10g
- *Fats:* 12g
- *Fiber:* 4g
- *Cholesterol:* 0mg
- *Sodium:* 200mg
- *Potassium:* 400mg

Grilled Asparagus with Lemon and Parmesan

Yield: 4 servings
Preparation Time: 10 minutes
Cooking Time: 8 minutes

Ingredients:

* 1 lb fresh asparagus, trimmed
* 2 tablespoons olive oil
* 1 teaspoon salt
* 1/2 teaspoon black pepper
* Juice of 1 lemon
* 1/4 cup grated Parmesan cheese
* Zest of 1 lemon (optional)
* Fresh parsley, chopped (for garnish)

Instructions:

1. Preheat the grill to medium-high heat and toss the asparagus with olive oil, salt, and pepper in a bowl until evenly coated.
2. Place the asparagus directly on the grill and cook for about 5-8 minutes, turning occasionally until tender and slightly charred.
3. Remove from the grill and drizzle with fresh lemon juice and zest, if using.
4. Sprinkle grated Parmesan cheese over the asparagus while still warm to allow it to melt slightly.
5. Garnish with fresh parsley before serving.

Nutritional Information (per serving):

* *Calories: 120*
* *Protein: 5g*
* *Carbohydrates: 6g*
* *Fats: 9g*
* *Fiber: 3g*
* *Cholesterol: 2mg*
* *Sodium: 250mg*
* *Potassium: 300mg*

Sautéed Spinach with Garlic and Olive Oil

Yield: 4 servings
Preparation Time: 5 minutes
Cooking Time: 5 minutes

Ingredients:

* 1 lb fresh spinach, washed and trimmed
* 3 tablespoons olive oil
* 3 cloves garlic, minced
* 1/4 teaspoon red pepper flakes (optional)
* Salt and pepper to taste
* Juice of 1/2 lemon
* Fresh lemon wedges (for serving)

Instructions:

1. Heat olive oil in a large skillet over medium heat, then add minced garlic and red pepper flakes, sautéing for about 1 minute until fragrant.
2. Add the spinach to the skillet, tossing to coat in the oil and garlic, and cook for 2-3 minutes until wilted.
3. Season with salt and pepper to taste, and squeeze fresh lemon juice over the spinach before removing from heat.
4. Continue to sauté for another minute, ensuring the spinach is well combined with the flavors.
5. Serve warm with lemon wedges on the side.

Nutritional Information (per serving):

* *Calories: 100*
* *Protein: 3g*
* *Carbohydrates: 4g*
* *Fats: 9g*
* *Fiber: 2g*
* *Cholesterol: 0mg*
* *Sodium: 150mg*
* *Potassium: 400mg*

Zucchini Boats with Tomatoes and Mozzarella

Yield: *4 servings*
Preparation Time: *15 minutes*
Cooking Time: *25 minutes*

Ingredients:

- 4 medium zucchinis
- 1 cup cherry tomatoes, halved
- 1 cup fresh mozzarella balls, halved (or shredded mozzarella)
- 2 tablespoons olive oil
- 1 teaspoon dried oregano
- 1 teaspoon salt
- 1/2 teaspoon black pepper
- Fresh basil for garnish

Instructions:
1. Preheat the oven to 375°F (190°C) and slice the zucchinis in half lengthwise, scooping out some flesh to create boats.
2. In a bowl, combine cherry tomatoes, mozzarella, olive oil, oregano, salt, and pepper; mix well.
3. Fill each zucchini boat with the tomato and mozzarella mixture, pressing down gently.
4. Place the stuffed zucchinis on a baking sheet and bake for 20-25 minutes, until the zucchinis are tender and the cheese is melted.
5. Garnish with fresh basil before serving.

Nutritional Information (per serving):
- *Calories: 200*
- *Protein: 10g*
- *Carbohydrates: 10g*
- *Fats: 14g*
- *Fiber: 3g*
- *Cholesterol: 30mg*
- *Sodium: 400mg*
- *Potassium: 400mg*

Roasted Brussels Sprouts with Pine Nuts

Yield: *4 servings*
Preparation Time: *10 minutes*
Cooking Time: *25 minutes*

Ingredients:

- 1 lb Brussels sprouts, trimmed and halved
- 3 tablespoons olive oil
- 1/2 teaspoon salt
- 1/4 teaspoon black pepper
- 1/4 cup pine nuts
- 1 tablespoon balsamic vinegar (optional)
- Fresh parsley, chopped (for garnish)

Instructions:

1. Preheat the oven to 400°F (200°C) and toss the halved Brussels sprouts with olive oil, salt, and pepper in a large bowl.
2. Spread the Brussels sprouts on a baking sheet in a single layer and roast for 20 minutes, stirring halfway through.
3. In the last 5 minutes of roasting, sprinkle pine nuts over the Brussels sprouts to toast.
4. Remove from the oven and drizzle with balsamic vinegar if using; toss to combine.
5. Garnish with fresh parsley before serving.

Nutritional Information (per serving):

- *Calories: 180*
- *Protein: 4g*
- *Carbohydrates: 10g*
- *Fats: 15g*
- *Fiber: 4g*
- *Cholesterol: 0mg*
- *Sodium: 200mg*
- *Potassium: 500mg*

Spinach and Feta Stuffed Mushrooms

Yield: 4 servings
Preparation Time: 15 minutes
Cooking Time: 20 minutes

Ingredients:

- 12 large portobello or cremini mushrooms, stems removed
- 2 cups fresh spinach, chopped
- 1/2 cup feta cheese, crumbled
- 1/4 cup cream cheese, softened
- 2 cloves garlic, minced
- 2 tablespoons olive oil
- 1/4 teaspoon salt
- 1/4 teaspoon black pepper
- 1 teaspoon dried oregano
- Fresh parsley, chopped (for garnish)

Instructions:

1. Preheat the oven to 375°F (190°C) and heat olive oil in a skillet over medium heat; add garlic and spinach, cooking until spinach is wilted.
2. In a bowl, mix cooked spinach, feta cheese, cream cheese, salt, pepper, and oregano until well combined.
3. Stuff each mushroom cap with the spinach and feta mixture, pressing down gently.
4. Place the stuffed mushrooms on a baking sheet and bake for 20 minutes until mushrooms are tender and tops are golden.
5. Garnish with fresh parsley before serving.

Nutritional Information (per serving):

- *Calories:* 180
- *Protein:* 8g
- *Carbohydrates:* 6g
- *Fats:* 15g
- *Fiber:* 2g
- *Cholesterol:* 30mg
- *Sodium:* 300mg
- *Potassium:* 400mg

Greek-Style Green Beans (Fasolakia)

Yield: 4 servings
Preparation Time: 10 minutes
Cooking Time: 30 minutes

Ingredients:

- 1 lb fresh green beans, trimmed
- 1/4 cup olive oil
- 1 medium onion, chopped
- 2 cloves garlic, minced
- 2 cups diced tomatoes (fresh or canned)
- 1 teaspoon dried oregano
- 1/2 teaspoon salt
- 1/4 teaspoon black pepper
- Juice of 1 lemon
- Fresh parsley, chopped (for garnish)

Instructions:

1. Heat olive oil in a large skillet over medium heat; add onion and garlic, sautéing until softened, about 5 minutes.
2. Add the green beans, diced tomatoes, oregano, salt, and pepper; stir well to combine.
3. Cover the skillet and simmer for 20-25 minutes, until the beans are tender, stirring occasionally.
4. Remove from heat and stir in lemon juice to enhance the flavors.
5. Garnish with fresh parsley before serving.

Nutritional Information (per serving):

- *Calories:* 180
- *Protein:* 3g
- *Carbohydrates:* 15g
- *Fats:* 13g
- *Fiber:* 5g
- *Cholesterol:* 0mg
- *Sodium:* 200mg
- *Potassium:* 400mg

Lemon Roasted Artichokes

Yield: *4 servings*
Preparation Time: *10 minutes*
Cooking Time: *40 minutes*

Ingredients:

- 4 medium artichokes
- 1/4 cup olive oil
- Juice of 2 lemons
- 4 cloves garlic, minced
- 1 teaspoon salt
- 1/2 teaspoon black pepper
- 1 teaspoon dried thyme (or fresh, if available)
- Fresh parsley, chopped (for garnish)

Instructions:

1. Preheat the oven to 400°F (200°C) and prepare the artichokes by trimming the stems and removing the tough outer leaves.
2. Cut each artichoke in half lengthwise and scoop out the fuzzy choke using a spoon.
3. In a bowl, whisk together olive oil, lemon juice, garlic, salt, pepper, and thyme; brush the mixture generously over the artichokes.
4. Place the artichokes cut side down on a baking sheet and roast for 30-35 minutes until tender and golden, flipping halfway through.
5. Garnish with fresh parsley before serving.

Nutritional Information (per serving):

- *Calories: 210*
- *Protein: 4g*
- *Carbohydrates: 18g*
- *Fats: 15g*
- *Fiber: 7g*
- *Cholesterol: 0mg*
- *Sodium: 300mg*
- *Potassium: 600mg*

Caramelized Carrots with Thyme and Honey

Yield: *4 servings*
Preparation Time: *10 minutes*
Cooking Time: *25 minutes*

Ingredients:

- 1 lb carrots, peeled and cut into 1-inch pieces
- 2 tablespoons olive oil
- 1 tablespoon honey
- 1 teaspoon fresh thyme leaves (or 1/2 teaspoon dried thyme)
- 1/2 teaspoon salt
- 1/4 teaspoon black pepper
- Fresh thyme sprigs for garnish (optional)

Instructions:

1. Preheat the oven to 400°F (200°C) and toss the carrot pieces with olive oil, honey, thyme, salt, and pepper in a large bowl.
2. Spread the carrots evenly on a baking sheet in a single layer.
3. Roast for 20-25 minutes, stirring halfway through, until the carrots are tender and caramelized.
4. Remove from the oven and let cool slightly to enhance the flavors.
5. Garnish with fresh thyme sprigs before serving.

Nutritional Information (per serving):

- *Calories: 150*
- *Protein: 1g*
- *Carbohydrates: 24g*
- *Fats: 7g*
- *Fiber: 4g*
- *Cholesterol: 0mg*
- *Sodium: 200mg*
- *Potassium: 450mg*

Moroccan Spiced Eggplant

Yield: 4 servings
Preparation Time: 15 minutes
Cooking Time: 30 minutes

Ingredients:

- 2 medium eggplants, cut into 1-inch cubes
- 3 tablespoons olive oil
- 1 teaspoon ground cumin
- 1 teaspoon ground coriander
- 1/2 teaspoon smoked paprika
- 1/2 teaspoon cinnamon
- 1/2 teaspoon salt
- 1/4 teaspoon black pepper
- 1 can (15 oz) diced tomatoes
- Fresh cilantro, chopped (for garnish)

Instructions:

1. Preheat the oven to 400°F (200°C) and toss the eggplant cubes with olive oil, cumin, coriander, paprika, cinnamon, salt, and pepper in a large bowl.
2. Spread the spiced eggplant evenly on a baking sheet and roast for 20 minutes, stirring halfway through until tender.
3. Add the diced tomatoes to the baking sheet, mixing well to combine, and roast for an additional 10 minutes.
4. Remove from the oven and let cool slightly to enhance the flavors.
5. Garnish with fresh cilantro before serving.

Nutritional Information (per serving):

- *Calories:* 180
- *Protein:* 4g
- *Carbohydrates:* 14g
- *Fats:* 12g
- *Fiber:* 6g
- *Cholesterol:* 0mg
- *Sodium:* 300mg
- *Potassium:* 600mg

Grilled Vegetable Platter with Hummus

Yield: 4 servings
Preparation Time: 15 minutes
Cooking Time: 15 minutes

Ingredients:

- 1 zucchini, sliced into rounds
- 1 bell pepper, cut into strips
- 1 red onion, sliced into rings
- 1 cup cherry tomatoes
- 1/4 cup olive oil
- 1 teaspoon dried oregano
- 1/2 teaspoon salt
- 1/4 teaspoon black pepper
- 1 cup hummus (store-bought or homemade)
- Fresh parsley, chopped (for garnish)

Instructions:

1. Preheat the grill to medium-high heat and toss the sliced vegetables with olive oil, oregano, salt, and pepper in a large bowl.
2. Grill the vegetables for about 3-5 minutes per side until tender and slightly charred.
3. Arrange the grilled vegetables on a serving platter.
4. Serve with hummus in the center, drizzling with olive oil if desired.
5. Garnish with fresh parsley before serving.

Nutritional Information (per serving):

- *Calories:* 200
- *Protein:* 6g
- *Carbohydrates:* 20g
- *Fats:* 12g
- *Fiber:* 5g
- *Cholesterol:* 0mg
- *Sodium:* 250mg
- *Potassium:* 450mg

Roasted Red Peppers with Olive Oil and Garlic

Yield: *4 servings*
Preparation Time: *10 minutes*
Cooking Time: *30 minutes*

Ingredients:

- 4 large red bell peppers
- 4 tablespoons olive oil
- 4 cloves garlic, thinly sliced
- 1 teaspoon salt
- 1/2 teaspoon black pepper
- 1 tablespoon balsamic vinegar (optional)
- Fresh basil or parsley, chopped (for garnish)

Instructions:

1. Preheat the oven to 425°F (220°C) and place the whole red peppers on a baking sheet.
2. Roast the peppers for 25-30 minutes, turning occasionally, until the skins are charred and blistered.
3. Remove the peppers from the oven and place them in a bowl, covering with plastic wrap to steam for 10 minutes; this makes peeling easier.
4. Once cooled, peel the skins off, slice the peppers into strips, and arrange them on a serving platter; drizzle with olive oil, garlic, salt, pepper, and balsamic vinegar if using.
5. Garnish with fresh herbs before serving.

Nutritional Information (per serving):

- *Calories: 150*
- *Protein: 2g*
- *Carbohydrates: 8g*
- *Fats: 14g*
- *Fiber: 2g*
- *Cholesterol: 0mg*
- *Sodium: 300mg*
- *Potassium: 400mg*

Stuffed Tomatoes with Rice and Herbs

Yield: *4 servings*
Preparation Time: *15 minutes*
Cooking Time: *30 minutes*

Ingredients:

- 4 large ripe tomatoes
- 1 cup cooked rice (white or brown)
- 1/2 cup diced onion
- 2 cloves garlic, minced
- 1/4 cup fresh parsley, chopped
- 1/4 cup fresh basil, chopped
- 1/4 teaspoon salt
- 1/4 teaspoon black pepper
- 2 tablespoons olive oil
- 1/4 cup grated Parmesan cheese (optional)

Instructions:

1. Preheat the oven to 375°F (190°C) and slice the tops off the tomatoes, scooping out the insides to create a hollow shell.
2. In a skillet, heat olive oil over medium heat, and sauté onion and garlic until softened; combine with cooked rice, herbs, salt, and pepper.
3. Stuff the rice mixture into the hollowed tomatoes, pressing gently to fill them completely.
4. Place the stuffed tomatoes in a baking dish, sprinkle with Parmesan cheese if desired, and bake for 25-30 minutes until the tomatoes are tender.
5. Serve warm, garnished with extra herbs if desired.

Nutritional Information (per serving):

- *Calories: 180*
- *Protein: 5g*
- *Carbohydrates: 28g*
- *Fats: 7g*
- *Fiber: 3g*
- *Cholesterol: 2mg*
- *Sodium: 200mg*
- *Potassium: 450mg*

CHAPTER 10: DESSERTS

Greek Baklava with Honey and Walnuts

Yield: 24 servings
Preparation Time: 30 minutes
Cooking Time: 45 minutes

Ingredients:

- 1 package (16 oz) phyllo dough, thawed
- 2 cups walnuts, finely chopped
- 1 teaspoon ground cinnamon
- 1 cup unsalted butter, melted
- 1 cup honey
- 1/2 cup granulated sugar
- 1 cup water
- 1 teaspoon vanilla extract
- 1/4 teaspoon salt

Instructions:

1. Preheat the oven to 350°F (175°C) and mix chopped walnuts with cinnamon in a bowl; set aside.
2. Brush a 9x13 inch baking dish with melted butter and layer 8 sheets of phyllo dough, brushing each with butter before adding the next.
3. Spread a third of the walnut mixture over the phyllo, then repeat the layering process (8 sheets of phyllo, butter, walnuts) two more times, finishing with 8 more phyllo sheets on top, brushing the final layer with butter.
4. Cut the baklava into diamond shapes and bake for 45 minutes until golden brown and crisp.
5. While baking, combine honey, sugar, water, vanilla, and salt in a saucepan; boil for 10 minutes, then pour over the hot baklava when it comes out of the oven.

Nutritional Information (per serving):

- *Calories: 230*
- *Protein: 3g*
- *Carbohydrates: 30g*
- *Fats: 12g*
- *Fiber: 1g*
- *Cholesterol: 20mg*
- *Sodium: 90mg*
- *Potassium: 100mg*

Olive Oil Cake with Lemon and Almonds

Yield: 8 servings
Preparation Time: 15 minutes
Cooking Time: 40 minutes

Ingredients:

- 1 cup extra virgin olive oil
- 1 cup granulated sugar
- 3 large eggs
- 1 cup almond flour
- 1 cup all-purpose flour
- 2 teaspoons baking powder
- 1/2 teaspoon salt
- Zest of 1 lemon
- 1/4 cup fresh lemon juice
- Powdered sugar (for dusting, optional)

Instructions:

1. Preheat the oven to 350°F (175°C) and grease an 8-inch round cake pan.
2. In a large bowl, whisk together olive oil and sugar until combined, then add eggs one at a time, mixing well after each addition.
3. In another bowl, combine almond flour, all-purpose flour, baking powder, salt, and lemon zest; gradually fold the dry ingredients into the wet mixture.
4. Stir in the lemon juice until just combined, then pour the batter into the prepared pan and smooth the top.
5. Bake for 35-40 minutes or until a toothpick inserted into the center comes out clean; cool before *dusting with powdered sugar.*

Nutritional Information (per serving):

- *Calories: 230*
- *Protein: 4g*
- *Carbohydrates: 29g*
- *Fats: 12g*
- *Fiber: 1g*
- *Cholesterol: 50mg*
- *Sodium: 150mg*
- *Potassium: 160mg*

Fig and Honey Tart

Yield: *8 servings*
Preparation Time: *20 minutes*
Cooking Time: *30 minutes*

Ingredients:

- 1 pre-made whole grain tart crust (9 inches)
- 1 cup fresh figs, sliced (about 10-12 figs)
- 1/2 cup ricotta cheese
- 1/4 cup honey, plus extra for drizzling
- 1 teaspoon vanilla extract
- 1/2 teaspoon cinnamon
- Fresh mint leaves for garnish (optional)

Instructions:

1. Preheat the oven to 375°F (190°C) and place the tart crust in a tart pan, pricking the bottom with a fork.
2. In a bowl, mix the ricotta cheese, honey, vanilla extract, and cinnamon until smooth; spread this mixture evenly over the tart crust.
3. Arrange the sliced figs on top of the ricotta mixture in a circular pattern.
4. Bake for 25-30 minutes until the crust is golden and the figs are softened; let cool for a few minutes.
5. *Drizzle with additional honey and garnish with fresh mint before serving.*

Nutritional Information (per serving):

- *Calories: 180*
- *Protein: 4g*
- *Carbohydrates: 28g*
- *Fats: 7g*
- *Fiber: 2g*
- *Cholesterol: 15mg*
- *Sodium: 100mg*
- *Potassium: 150mg*

Pistachio and Rose Water Ice Cream

Yield: *6 servings*
Preparation Time: *15 minutes (plus freezing time)*
Cooking Time: *0 minutes*

Ingredients:

- 2 cups unsweetened almond milk (or whole milk)
- 1 cup heavy cream
- 1/2 cup granulated sugar
- 1/2 cup shelled pistachios, finely chopped (plus extra for garnish)
- 2 teaspoons rose water
- 1/2 teaspoon vanilla extract
- Pinch of salt

Instructions:

1. In a mixing bowl, whisk together the almond milk, heavy cream, sugar, rose water, vanilla extract, and salt until the sugar is dissolved.
2. Stir in the finely chopped pistachios, ensuring they are evenly distributed.
3. Pour the mixture into an ice cream maker and churn according to the manufacturer's instructions until it reaches a soft-serve consistency (about 20-25 minutes).
4. Transfer the ice cream to a lidded container and freeze for at least 4 hours or until firm.
5. Serve scoops of the ice cream garnished with additional pistachios.

Nutritional Information (per serving):

- *Calories: 220*
- *Protein: 3g*
- *Carbohydrates: 20g*
- *Fats: 15g*
- *Fiber: 1g*
- *Cholesterol: 40mg*
- *Sodium: 50mg*
- *Potassium: 180mg*

Greek Yogurt with Honey and Fresh Berries

Yield: 4 servings
Preparation Time: 10 minutes
Cooking Time: 0 minutes

Ingredients:

- 4 cups plain Greek yogurt (full-fat or low-fat)
- 1 cup mixed fresh berries (e.g., strawberries, blueberries, raspberries)
- 1/4 cup honey (or to taste)
- 1/4 teaspoon vanilla extract (optional)
- Mint leaves for garnish (optional)

Instructions:

1. In a serving bowl or individual cups, divide the Greek yogurt evenly among four servings.
2. Drizzle each serving with honey, adjusting the amount to your sweetness preference.
3. Top the yogurt with a generous handful of mixed fresh berries.
4. If using, add a drop of vanilla extract to enhance the flavor.
5. Garnish with mint leaves and serve immediately.

Nutritional Information (per serving):

- *Calories:* 210
- *Protein:* 14g
- *Carbohydrates:* 34g
- *Fats:* 5g
- *Fiber:* 3g
- *Cholesterol:* 15mg
- *Sodium:* 70mg
- *Potassium:* 300mg

Lemon and Poppy Seed Cookies

Yield: 24 cookies
Preparation Time: 15 minutes
Cooking Time: 12-15 minutes

Ingredients:

- 1 1/2 cups almond flour
- 1/2 cup coconut flour
- 1/2 cup granulated sugar (or coconut sugar)
- 1/4 cup honey or maple syrup
- 2 large eggs
- Zest of 1 lemon
- 2 tablespoons lemon juice
- 2 tablespoons poppy seeds
- 1 teaspoon baking powder
- 1/4 teaspoon salt
- Optional: 1/2 teaspoon vanilla extract

Instructions:

1. Preheat the oven to 350°F (175°C) and line a baking sheet with parchment paper.
2. In a large bowl, mix the almond flour, coconut flour, sugar, baking powder, and salt.
3. In another bowl, whisk together the eggs, honey (or maple syrup), lemon zest, lemon juice, and vanilla extract (if using).
4. Combine the wet and dry ingredients, then fold in the poppy seeds until just mixed.
5. Drop tablespoonfuls of dough onto the prepared baking sheet and bake for 12-15 minutes until lightly *golden; let cool before serving.*

Nutritional Information (per cookie):

- *Calories:* 120
- *Protein:* 3g
- *Carbohydrates:* 10g
- *Fats:* 8g
- *Fiber:* 2g
- *Cholesterol:* 30mg
- *Sodium:* 50mg
- *Potassium:* 100mg

Date and Almond Energy Bites

Yield: *12 energy bites*
Preparation Time: *10 minutes*
Cooking Time: *0 minutes*

Ingredients:

- 1 cup Medjool dates, pitted
- 1 cup almonds (or almond flour for a smoother texture)
- 1/4 cup rolled oats
- 1 tablespoon chia seeds (optional)
- 1 tablespoon almond butter (or any nut butter)
- 1 teaspoon vanilla extract
- Pinch of sea salt
- Optional: 1/2 teaspoon cinnamon or cocoa powder for flavor

Instructions:

1. In a food processor, combine the pitted dates, almonds, oats, chia seeds, almond butter, vanilla extract, and salt until a sticky mixture forms.
2. If desired, add cinnamon or cocoa powder for extra flavor and pulse to combine.
3. Roll the mixture into small balls (about 1 inch in diameter) and place them on a plate.
4. Refrigerate for at least 30 minutes to firm up the bites.
5. Serve chilled or at room temperature as a nutritious snack.

Nutritional Information (per energy bite):
- *Calories: 100*
- *Protein: 3g*
- *Carbohydrates: 12g*
- *Fats: 5g*
- *Fiber: 2g*
- *Cholesterol: 0mg*
- *Sodium: 1mg*
- *Potassium: 150mg*

Honey and Walnut Phyllo Rolls

Yield: *12 rolls*
Preparation Time: *20 minutes*
Cooking Time: *25 minutes*

Ingredients:

- 8 sheets of phyllo dough
- 1 cup walnuts, chopped
- 1/4 cup honey
- 1/2 teaspoon cinnamon (optional)
- 1/4 cup melted olive oil or butter
- Pinch of salt

Instructions:

1. Preheat the oven to 350°F (175°C) and line a baking sheet with parchment paper.
2. In a bowl, mix chopped walnuts, honey, cinnamon, and a pinch of salt until well combined.
3. Place one sheet of phyllo dough on a clean surface, brush lightly with melted olive oil, and layer with another sheet; repeat this twice for a total of three layers.
4. Place a generous tablespoon of the walnut mixture at one end, roll tightly, and seal the edges with olive oil.
5. Arrange the rolls on the baking sheet, brush the tops with olive oil, and bake for 20-25 minutes until golden brown.

Nutritional Information (per roll):
- *Calories: 150*
- *Protein: 3g*
- *Carbohydrates: 15g*
- *Fats: 9g*
- *Fiber: 1g*
- *Cholesterol: 0mg*
- *Sodium: 50mg*
- *Potassium: 100mg*

Chocolate Olive Oil Cake

Yield: *8 servings*
Preparation Time: *15 minutes*
Cooking Time: *35 minutes*

Ingredients:

- 1 cup all-purpose flour
- 1/2 cup unsweetened cocoa powder
- 1 teaspoon baking powder
- 1/2 teaspoon baking soda
- 1/4 teaspoon salt
- 1/2 cup granulated sugar
- 2 large eggs
- 1/2 cup extra virgin olive oil
- 1/2 cup almond milk (or any milk)
- 1 teaspoon vanilla extract
- Optional: powdered sugar for dusting

Instructions:

1. Preheat the oven to 350°F (175°C) and grease an 8-inch round cake pan.
2. In a bowl, whisk together flour, cocoa powder, baking powder, baking soda, and salt; set aside.
3. In a separate bowl, beat together sugar and eggs until light, then mix in olive oil, almond milk, and vanilla.
4. Gradually add the dry ingredients to the wet ingredients, mixing until just combined.
5. Pour the batter into the prepared pan and bake for 30-35 minutes or until a toothpick inserted in the center comes out clean.

Nutritional Information (per serving):

- *Calories: 180*
- *Protein: 4g*
- *Carbohydrates: 25g*
- *Fats: 8g*
- *Fiber: 2g*
- *Cholesterol: 30mg*
- *Sodium: 120mg*
- *Potassium: 150mg*

Semolina Cake with Orange Syrup (Revani)

Yield: *10 servings*
Preparation Time: *15 minutes*
Cooking Time: *35 minutes*

Ingredients:

- **For the Cake:**
  - 1 cup semolina
  - 1 cup granulated sugar
  - 1 cup plain yogurt
  - 1/2 cup olive oil
  - 3 large eggs
  - 1 teaspoon baking powder
  - Zest of 1 orange
- **For the Orange Syrup:**
  - 1 cup water
  - 1 cup granulated sugar
  - Juice of 1 orange
  - 1 teaspoon vanilla extract

Instructions:

1. Preheat the oven to 350°F (175°C) and grease a 9x13 inch baking dish.
2. In a large bowl, whisk together semolina, sugar, yogurt, olive oil, eggs, baking powder, and orange zest until smooth.
3. Pour the batter into the prepared dish and bake for 30-35 minutes until golden and a toothpick comes out clean.
4. While the cake is baking, prepare the syrup by boiling water, sugar, orange juice, and vanilla in a saucepan for about 10 minutes until slightly thickened.
5. Once the cake is done, pour the warm syrup over it and let it absorb for at least 30 minutes before serving.

Nutritional Information (per serving):

- *Calories: 220*
- *Protein: 4g*
- *Carbohydrates: 35g*
- *Fats: 8g*
- *Fiber: 1g*
- *Cholesterol: 40mg*
- *Sodium: 90mg*
- *Potassium: 150mg*

Tahini and Honey Cookies

Yield: 12 cookies
Preparation Time: 10 minutes
Cooking Time: 15 minutes

Ingredients:

- 1 cup tahini (unsweetened)
- 1/2 cup honey
- 1/4 cup almond flour
- 1/2 teaspoon baking soda
- 1/4 teaspoon salt
- 1 teaspoon vanilla extract
- Optional: 1/2 teaspoon cinnamon or chopped nuts for added flavor

Instructions:

1. Preheat the oven to 350°F (175°C) and line a baking sheet with parchment paper.
2. In a bowl, mix tahini, honey, almond flour, baking soda, salt, and vanilla extract until smooth; add cinnamon or nuts if desired.
3. Scoop tablespoon-sized amounts of dough onto the prepared baking sheet, spacing them apart.
4. Flatten each cookie slightly with the back of a fork and bake for 12-15 minutes until lightly golden.
5. Allow to cool on the baking sheet for a few minutes before transferring to a wire rack to cool completely.

Nutritional Information (per cookie):

- *Calories: 120*
- *Protein: 3g*
- *Carbohydrates: 9g*
- *Fats: 8g*
- *Fiber: 1g*
- *Cholesterol: 0mg*
- *Sodium: 60mg*
- *Potassium: 100mg*

Ricotta Cheesecake with Fresh Berries

Yield: 8 servings
Preparation Time: 20 minutes
Cooking Time: 45 minutes

Ingredients:

- 1 ½ cups ricotta cheese (drained)
- 1/2 cup Greek yogurt
- 1/3 cup honey or maple syrup
- 3 large eggs
- 1 teaspoon vanilla extract
- 1 teaspoon lemon zest
- 1/4 cup almond flour (for crust)
- 1/4 cup unsalted butter (melted)
- Fresh berries (strawberries, blueberries, raspberries) for topping

Instructions:

1. Preheat the oven to 350°F (175°C) and grease a 9-inch springform pan.
2. In a bowl, combine ricotta, Greek yogurt, honey, eggs, vanilla extract, and lemon zest until smooth; pour into the prepared pan.
3. In another bowl, mix almond flour with melted butter and press into the bottom of the pan to form a crust.
4. Bake for 40-45 minutes until the center is set and lightly golden; let cool in the pan for 10 minutes before removing.
5. Top with fresh berries before serving, and chill in the refrigerator for an hour for the best texture.

Nutritional Information (per serving):

- *Calories: 180*
- *Protein: 8g*
- *Carbohydrates: 15g*
- *Fats: 10g*
- *Fiber: 1g*
- *Cholesterol: 80mg*
- *Sodium: 70mg*
- *Potassium: 150mg*

Roasted Pears with Cinnamon and Honey

Yield: 4 servings
Preparation Time: 10 minutes
Cooking Time: 25 minutes

Ingredients:

- 4 ripe pears, halved and cored
- 2 tablespoons honey
- 1 teaspoon ground cinnamon
- 1 tablespoon olive oil
- 1 tablespoon lemon juice
- Optional: chopped walnuts or almonds for topping

Instructions:

1. Preheat the oven to 375°F (190°C) and line a baking sheet with parchment paper.
2. In a bowl, mix honey, olive oil, lemon juice, and cinnamon, then brush the mixture over the pear halves.
3. Place the pears cut-side up on the baking sheet and roast for 25 minutes until tender and caramelized.
4. Optional: sprinkle with chopped walnuts or almonds during the last 5 minutes of roasting for added crunch.
5. Serve warm as a dessert or snack, drizzled with extra honey if desired.

Nutritional Information (per serving):

- *Calories:* 150
- *Protein:* 1g
- *Carbohydrates:* 38g
- *Fats:* 2g
- *Fiber:* 5g
- *Cholesterol:* 0mg
- *Sodium:* 1mg
- *Potassium:* 190mg

Almond Biscotti with Dark Chocolate

Yield: 16 biscotti
Preparation Time: 15 minutes
Cooking Time: 35 minutes

Ingredients:

- 1 cup whole almonds, toasted
- 2 cups almond flour
- 1/2 cup whole wheat flour
- 1/2 cup honey or maple syrup
- 2 large eggs
- 1 teaspoon vanilla extract
- 1/2 teaspoon baking powder
- 1/4 teaspoon salt
- 4 oz dark chocolate, chopped (70% cocoa or higher)

Instructions:

1. Preheat the oven to 350°F (175°C) and line a baking sheet with parchment paper.
2. In a large bowl, mix almond flour, whole wheat flour, baking powder, and salt; then add honey, eggs, and vanilla, mixing until combined. Fold in the toasted almonds.
3. Shape the dough into a log on the baking sheet and bake for 25 minutes; cool for 10 minutes before slicing into 1/2-inch pieces.
4. Place the biscotti cut-side down on the baking sheet and bake for an additional 10 minutes until golden and crisp.
5. Melt the dark chocolate and dip the cooled biscotti, then let them set on parchment paper.

Nutritional Information (per biscotti):

- *Calories:* 110
- *Protein:* 3g
- *Carbohydrates:* 13g
- *Fats:* 5g
- *Fiber:* 1g
- *Cholesterol:* 0mg
- *Sodium:* 30mg
- *Potassium:* 100mg

Mediterranean Fruit Salad with Mint

Yield: 6 servings
Preparation Time: 15 minutes
Cooking Time: 0 minutes

Ingredients:

- 2 cups watermelon, diced
- 2 cups cantaloupe, diced
- 1 cup strawberries, sliced
- 1 cup blueberries
- 1 cup grapes, halved
- 1/4 cup fresh mint leaves, chopped
- Juice of 1 lemon
- 1 tablespoon honey (optional)

Instructions:

1. In a large bowl, combine the diced watermelon, cantaloupe, strawberries, blueberries, and grapes.
2. In a small bowl, whisk together the lemon juice and honey (if using) until well combined.
3. Drizzle the lemon dressing over the fruit and gently toss to coat.
4. Add the chopped mint leaves and toss lightly again to combine.
5. Serve immediately or refrigerate for up to 30 minutes to enhance flavors.

Nutritional Information (per serving):

- *Calories:* 80
- *Protein:* 1g
- *Carbohydrates:* 20g
- *Fats:* 0g
- *Fiber:* 2g
- *Cholesterol:* 0mg
- *Sodium:* 5mg
- *Potassium:* 150mg

MASTERING THE MEDITERRANEAN DIET: PRACTICAL TIPS AND TECHNIQUES FOR SUCCESS

The Mediterranean Diet is more than just a way of eating; it's a lifestyle rich in flavors, nutrients, and cultural traditions that promote long-term health. By incorporating fresh, wholesome ingredients and following a few practical strategies, you can enjoy the numerous benefits this diet offers. This guide provides effective techniques, tips, and tricks to help you maximize your success and enjoyment while adhering to the principles of the Mediterranean Diet.

Meal Planning: Crafting a Balanced Menu

Weekly Menu Strategies

1. **Balance Your Nutrients**:
    o **Proteins**: include lean sources such as fish, chicken, legumes, and nuts.
    o **Grains**: opt for whole grains like quinoa, brown rice, and whole-grain pasta.
    o **Vegetables**: fill half your plate with colorful vegetables to maximize nutrients.
2. **Variety is Key**: plan different meals for each day to keep your diet interesting. For example:
    o **Monday**: grilled chicken with roasted vegetables and quinoa.
    o **Tuesday**: lentil soup with a side of whole-grain bread.
    o **Wednesday**: baked salmon with a Mediterranean salad.
3. **Theme Days**: designate specific days for certain themes, such as Meatless Monday or Fish Friday, to encourage variety and creativity in your meals.

Tools and Apps for Planning

- **Meal Planning Apps**: utilize apps like **Paprika**, **MyFitnessPal**, or **Yummly** to help you create weekly menus, track food intake, and save favorite recipes.
- **Template for Meal Planning**: greate a simple weekly template to fill in your meals, which can help you stay organized and reduce food waste.

Grocery Shopping: Smart Strategies

Efficient Shopping Techniques

1. **Create a Shopping List**: before heading to the store, draft a list based on your meal plan to stay focused and avoid impulse purchases.
2. **Shop the Perimeter**: typically, fresh produce, meats, and dairy products are located around the outer edges of grocery stores. Focus your shopping here to find whole, unprocessed foods.

Choosing Fresh and Nutritious Options

- **Fruits and Vegetables**: select seasonal produce for the best flavor and price. Look for vibrant colors and firm textures when choosing fruits and vegetables.
- **Whole Grains**: read labels to ensure you choose whole grain options. Look for products that list whole grain as the first ingredient.
- **Nuts and Seeds**: opt for unsalted varieties to control sodium intake.

Cost-Saving Tips

- **Buy in Bulk**: purchase grains, nuts, and legumes in bulk to save money. Store them in airtight containers to maintain freshness.
- **Frozen Fruits and Vegetables**: frozen options can be just as nutritious and are often less expensive, making them great for smoothies or quick stir-fries.

Cooking Techniques for the Mediterranean Diet

1. **Grilling** - this method enhances the natural flavors of foods without the need for excessive oils. Grill vegetables, chicken, and fish for delicious results.
2. **Roasting** - roasting brings out the sweetness in vegetables. Drizzle them with olive oil, sprinkle with herbs, and roast until tender.
3. **Sautéing** - use olive oil or vegetable broth to sauté vegetables, allowing them to retain their nutrients and flavor.

Use fresh herbs like basil, oregano, and parsley liberally. They add flavor without extra calories or sodium.

Adopting the Mediterranean Diet is not just about changing what you eat; it's about embracing a healthier, more flavorful lifestyle. By implementing the techniques and strategies outlined in this guide—meal planning, grocery shopping, cooking, and navigating social situations—you can confidently embark on your Mediterranean journey.

Remember to enjoy the process, experiment with new flavors, and celebrate your progress as you make positive changes to your eating habits. The Mediterranean Diet can lead to a richer, healthier life, and every step you take towards this lifestyle is a step towards greater well-being.

MEAL PLANS

1 WEEK

	BREAKFAST	LUNCH	DINNER
MON	Mediterranean Spinach and Feta Omelette	Arugula Salad with Lemon and Parmesan	Grilled Lemon Herb Shrimp Skewers
TUE	Greek Yogurt and Honey Parfait	Tomato and Cucumber Salad with Fresh Herbs	Beef and Vegetable Moussaka
WEN	Za'atar-Spiced Breakfast Pita	Fennel and Orange Salad with Olives	Baked Cod with Olive and Tomato Relish
THU	Shakshuka with Fresh Herbs	Spinach and Pomegranate Salad with Walnuts	Garlic and Herb Crusted Pork Tenderloin
FRI	Lemon Ricotta Pancakes with Berries	Lentil Salad with Feta and Mint	Chicken with Olives and Artichokes
SAT	Avocado and Hummus Toast	Couscous Salad with Roasted Vegetables	Spicy Lamb Meatballs with Yogurt Sauce
SUN	Olive Oil Fried Eggs with Spinach and Tomatoes	Avocado and Tomato Mediterranean Salad	Pomegranate Glazed Chicken Thighs

MEAL PLANS
2 WEEK

	BREAKFAST	LUNCH	DINNER
MON	Olive Oil Fried Eggs with Spinach and Tomatoes	Chicken and Chickpea Stew with Spinach	Baked Salmon with Spinach and Feta
TUE	Labneh with Pistachios and Pomegranate	Seared Scallops with Herb Butter	Zucchini Boats with Tomatoes and Mozzarella
WEN	Smoked Salmon Breakfast Bagel	Bulgur with Herbs and Pine Nuts	Mediterranean Chicken and Orzo Bake
THU	Mediterranean Breakfast Burrito	Garlic Roasted Pork Shoulder	Red Snapper with Olives and Capers
FRI	Roasted Red Pepper and Goat Cheese Frittata	Balsamic Chicken with Roasted Tomatoes	Tomato and Basil Risotto
SAT	Spanish Tortilla with Potatoes and Onions	Eggplant and Olive Baked Pasta	Roasted Brussels Sprouts with Pine Nuts
SUN	Fig and Walnut Oatmeal	Grilled Sardines with Lemon and Rosemary	Spicy Chicken Shawarma Wraps

MEAL PLANS

3 WEEK

	BREAKFAST	LUNCH	DINNER
MON	Labneh with Pistachios and Pomegranate	Roasted Red Pepper and Artichoke Salad	Saffron Mussels with Garlic and White Wine
TUE	Smoked Salmon Breakfast Bagel	Farro Salad with Sun-Dried Tomatoes	Shrimp and Artichoke Pasta
WEN	Mediterranean Breakfast Burrito	Eggplant and Tomato Salad with Fresh Basil	Lemon Garlic Chicken Skewers
THU	Roasted Red Pepper and Goat Cheese Frittata	Spicy Lamb Meatballs with Yogurt Sauce	Seared Scallops with Herb Butter
FRI	Spanish Tortilla with Potatoes and Onions	Beef Shawarma with Garlic Sauce	Braised Beef with Olives and Tomatoes
SAT	Fig and Walnut Oatmeal	Braised Beef with Olives and Tomatoes	Baked Salmon with Spinach and Feta
SUN	Tomato and Olive Breakfast Bruschetta	Mediterranean Stuffed Bell Peppers with Lamb	Mediterranean Stuffed Bell Peppers with Lamb

MEAL PLANS

4 WEEK

	BREAKFAST	LUNCH	DINNER
MON	Almond and Orange Scones	Herb-Marinated Grilled Steak	Herb-Crusted Chicken Breasts
TUE	Baked Eggs with Spinach and Tomatoes	Pork Souvlaki with Lemon Potatoes	Herb-Marinated Grilled Steak

WEN	Za'atar-Spiced Breakfast Pita	Grilled Vegetable Platter with Hummus	Grilled Sardines with Lemon and Rosemary
THU	Shakshuka with Fresh Herbs	Moroccan Carrot Salad with Cumin and Coriander	Pork Souvlaki with Lemon Potatoes
FRI	Lemon Ricotta Pancakes with Berries	Grilled Halloumi and Watermelon Salad	Mediterranean Fish Stew with Saffron
SAT	Avocado and Hummus Toast	Roasted Beet Salad with Goat Cheese	Greek Meatball Soup (Youvarlakia)
SUN	Olive Oil Fried Eggs with Spinach and Tomatoes	Chickpea Salad with Cucumber and Red Onion	Garlic and Lemon Baked Tilapia
MON	Labneh with Pistachios and Pomegranate	Tabouleh with Fresh Mint and Lemon	Shrimp Saganaki with Tomatoes and Feta
TUE	Lemon Ricotta Pancakes with Berries	Classic Greek Salad with Feta and Olives	Balsamic Glazed Lamb Chops

Made in United States
Troutdale, OR
12/29/2024

27392973R10058